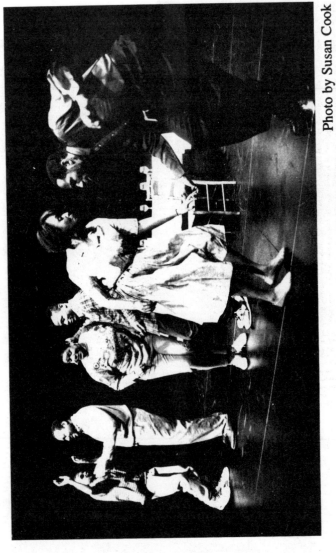

Photo by Susan Cook

A Scene from the Second Stage Theatre production of "Before It Hits Home." Set design by Loy Arcenas.

BEFORE IT HITS HOME

BY CHERYL L. WEST

★

DRAMATISTS
PLAY SERVICE
INC.

BEFORE IT HITS HOME
Copyright © 1993, Cheryl L. West

All Rights Reserved

SPECIAL NOTE

Workshopped by the Seattle Group Theatre in conjunction with its Multicultural Playwrights' Festival, Seattle Washington, 1989.

This play was given readings at Circle Repertory Company.

BEFORE IT HITS HOME was produced in 1991 by Arena Stage, Zelda Fichhandler, Producing Director, as part of the NBC "New Voices" Program.

Original New York Production by Second Stage Theatre, Robyn Goodman and Carole Rothman, Artistic Directors, on March 10, 1992.

This play is dedicated to those who have to hide
and to those who refuse to

BEFORE IT HITS HOME was produced by Second Stage Theatre (Robyn Goodman and Carole Rothman, Artistic Directors) in New York City, in March, 1992. It was directed by Tazewell Thompson; the set design was by Loy Arcenas; the costumes design was by Paul Tazewell; the lighting design was by Nancy Schertler; the sound design was by Susan R. White and the production manager was Carol Fishman. The cast was as follows:

WENDAL ....James McDaniel
SIMONE, MISS PETERSON ....Sharon Washington
DOUGLASS ....Keith Randolph Smith
REBA ....Yvette Hawkins
MAYBELLE ....Marcella Lowery
BAILEY..Frankie R. Faison
DWAYNE ....James Jason Lilley
NURSE ....Carol Honda
DR. WEINBERG..Beth Dixon
JUNIOR ....Monti Sharp

BEFORE IT HITS HOME was produced by Arena Stage (Zelda Fichandler, Producing Director) as part of the NBC "New Voices" Program, in Washington, D.C., in January, 1991. It was directed by Tazewell Thompson; the set design was by Douglas Stein; the lighting design was by Nancy Schertler; the costume design was by Helen Qizhi Huang; the sound design was by Susan R. White and the stage manager was Wendy Streeter. The cast was as follows:

WENDAL ....Michael Jayce
SIMONE, MRS. PETERSON ....Cynthia Martells
DOUGLAS ....Keith Randolph Smith
REBA ....Trazana Beverley
NURSE ....Mercedes Herrero
MAYBELLE ....Sandra Reaves-Phillips
DOCTOR ....Julian Hughes
BAILEY..Walley Taylor
DWAYNE ....Ryan Richmond
JUNIOR..Lee Simon, Jr.

4

BEFORE IT HITS HOME was workshopped by the Seattle Group Theatre in conjunction with its Multicultural Playwrights' Festival, in Seattle, Washington, 1989. It was later given a reading at Circle Repertory Company, in New York City, in 1990.

CHARACTERS

WENDAL, Black male in his early 30s
REBA, Black woman in her 50s, Wendal's mother
BAILEY, Black man in his late 50s, Wendal's father
MAYBELLE, Black woman in her 50s, Reba's best friend
SIMONE, Black woman in her early 20s. Wendal's lover
ANGEL PETERSON, Black woman in her early 20s, Woman in clinic
DOUGLASS, Black man in his early 40s, Wendal's lover
JUNIOR, Black male in his late 20s, Wendal's younger brother
DWAYNE, Black boy, 12, Wendal's son
DOCTOR, White woman in her 40s or 50s
NURSE, a middle-age Hispanic or Asian woman

** The following part is played by the above:
ANGEL PETERSON (should be played by whomever
    plays Simone)
TWO ATTENDANTS (Attendants can be used as part of the crew, but their primary actions are to assist Wendal on stage.)

AUTHOR'S NOTE

There is a tendency to be seduced by the Bailey family, thus having the focus of the play be on them. This is not my intention. Wendal's two worlds — before he gets home and after he gets home — are equally important and at times, equally fractured. Douglass and Simone are not "social" characters and should not be portrayed as such. The action shifts frequently and the pacing between scenes should be quick, and in some scenes (as noted), action juxtaposed. To expedite this, whenever possible, actors should remain on stage while other scenes are taking place and remain true to the overlapping dialogue in the play.

BEFORE IT HITS HOME

PROLOGUE

Wendal is in a bar playing his saxophone. Wendal is in to it, feeling the power, his power. Each note punctuates how "bad" he is. He's one fine confident specimen.

Sound cue of audience clapping.

WENDAL. Thank you. Thank you. I dedicate that song for a special lady, Mrs. Reba Bailey, and since today is her birthday and I can't be with her ... that one's for you Mama. You know we talk about first love, but we got it wrong. I'm here to tell you, your first love connection is Mama, that first love journey is with her. And usually it's the one kinda love that out lasts the test of time. Home boy over there says I heard that. *(Chuckles.)* I know that's right. Don't get me wrong, I love my woman, I ain't no Oedipus or some sick shit like that, but I ain't shamed to tell you, I got one of them Sadie Mamas. Can't touch her. Yeah, you know what I'm talkin' 'bout. So happy birthday Mama ... *(Coughs.)* This next tune, a ballad. We're gonna play it deep, deep as your Mama's soul ... *(He plays saxophone again.)*

SIMONE. *(Crosses.)* Baby I told you that cough is getting worse. Flu doesn't hang on this long. Do I need to call the doctor for you? Is that what you're waiting on? Ok, Simone's going to call the doctor for her big baby. Make him an appointment ... but mister baby better take his sick behind down there. No more excuses Wendal. Ok? *(Suggestively.)* Hey baby

9

it's been a while.... Do I have to start hanging my panties out to dry on your horn? *(Simone exits.)*

WENDAL.   For those of you who don't know, I'm Wendal Bailey and we're Sojourn. We're glad you came out tonight. Fellas and me gon' take a short break. So, have another drink, don't forget to tip the ladies and we'll be right back at you. *(Just then Douglass strikes a match, lights a cigarette. Wendal crosses to Douglass and takes a drag off of Douglass's cigarette, silence for a moment. The silence is not awkward; instead these are two people used to communicating in whatever form, even abbreviated, if and when their environment dictates to do such.)*

DOUGLASS.   You have any time later?

WENDAL.   I don't know. I promised Simone I'd be home early. Breaks over. You gon' wait around?

DOUGLASS.   Probably. I liked that last song. What's the name of it?

WENDAL.   Hell if I know. The shit defies a title. If you knew my old girl, you'd know what I mean. *(Wendal starts to play, his sound is eerie in its need, its desperation.)*

ACT ONE

Clinic reception area. Sound of Wendal singing before lights. Waiting is a very pregnant Angel Peterson. A half-finished lunch is at her side. She is tired looking, haggard. Nurse is sitting at the desk.

ANGEL.   *(Slamming the magazine.)* How long she gon' be? I can't be sitting up here all day.

NURSE.   Like I told you before Ms. Peterson, the doctor will be with you as soon as possible.

ANGEL.   That's what you said two hours ago. *(Grumbling to herself.)* All day sittin' up in somebody's f'ing clinic, with nothing to look at but you white folks.

NURSE.   Ms. Peterson, first of all I'm not white.

ANGEL.   Same difference. *(Wendal enters loudly singing; so cool — so full of himself.)*

WENDAL.   *(To Nurse.)* Excuse me, I have an appointment with a Dr. Weinberg. Bailey ...

NURSE.   Yes ... you can fill out this medical history form *(Hands him a clipboard.)* and the doctor will be with you in a few minutes.

ANGEL.   She lying.

WENDAL.   *(To Angel.)* What's up? How you doing?

ANGEL.   Hangin'. *(Wendal sits, works on the clipboard, starts humming and singing again. After a moment, to Wendal.)* Hey. *(Louder.)* Hey. Yeah, I'm talking to you cutie pie. This first time here?

WENDAL.   Un-hum.

ANGEL.   Could tell. You too damn happy to be in the family. *(Pause.)* Taurus!

WENDAL.   What?

ANGEL.   Naw don't tell me. Sag, Cancer, Gemini ... Gemini! You's a Gemini if I ever saw one. My old man was a Gemini. All you fine mutherfuckers are Geminis. Can tell by the way

11

you walk. You think yo shit don't stink.

WENDAL.   Scorpio. And I been told my shit smells better than most colognes, 'specially them expensive kind.

ANGEL.   *(Laughs.)* Umph! I heard that. *(Wendal laughs too.)* Man, what's your name?

WENDAL.   Wendal. Wendal Bailey.

ANGEL.   My name Angel. Angel Peterson.

WENDAL.   *(Eyeing her stomach.)* So when's the big day?

ANGEL.   Soon. Just holdin' on till it gits here, then I'm gittin' on board, catching the first thing smokin' 'tween this hell and heaven's door. *(Angel has a coughing fit, Wendal hands her a handkerchief. She wipes her mouth, then takes out a compact and lipstick, applies make-up, a little too much, which gives her a garish appearance. She continues while looking in the compact mirror.)* I don't know what I'd do without this shit. *(Re: Make-up.)* How I look?

WENDAL.   Fine.

ANGEL.   You ain't a good liar Wendal Bailey. See the secret is they don't seem to find as much wrong with you when you look pretty. *(Holds out the compact to him.)* You wanna try some?

WENDAL.   I'll pass.

ANGEL.   So Mr. Shit-smell-better-than-cologne, what you here to see the AIDS doctor for?

WENDAL.   Who said who I was here to see? What I'm here for ain't really none of your business....

ANGEL.   Oh-oh. Got me a live one here. I love you first-time boys. Some indignant mutherfuckers. Well you better come offa that pride Mr. Bailey, 'cause you gon' git your feelings hurt ... *(Yelling to Nurse.)* Tell this sick mutherfucker he's got AIDS and put him out of his misery ... so he can stop walking around foolin' himself ...

NURSE.   Ms. Peterson ... we do not discuss a patients medical history with another patient.

WENDAL.   You got a nasty mouth on you, you know that?

ANGEL.   Un-hun ... it finally caught up with the rest of me.

WENDAL.   Well I don't appreciate it.

ANGEL.   Me neither. *(A beat.)* Solid. I was just trying to help you out brother. Welcome you into the family.

WENDAL. What are you talking about? What family?

ANGEL. You'll see ...

NURSE. Ms. Peterson, you can come in now ...

ANGEL. I'll see you around ...

WENDAL. I doubt it....

ANGEL. Oh yeah, we'll see each other again ... just like the train ... there's always a new one coming in and another one going out ... (*She exits singing the same song Wendal was singing when he entered. Nurse looks at Wendal. Wendal starts to laugh. It is an uneasy laugh.*)

WENDAL. She's a trip. (*Laughs again.*) I don't think the chick's playing with a full deck. Kept calling me part of some family. (*Laughs again as his laugh fades into Reba's and Maybelle's laughter. Fade in to Bailey household. Maybelle is in the mirror trying to see her backside. Reba is standing behind her.*)

MAYBELLE. I don't see what you talkin' about Reba ...

REBA. That's because you don't wanna see ...

MAYBELLE. That ain't nothing ... nothing but a curve.

REBA. Well that curve is ten pounds with dimples. You oughtta get here early so you can get on the floor with me and do some exercise.

MAYBELLE. That floor is hard.

REBA. And so is your head.

MAYBELLE. (*Pouting.*) I don't 'preciate you talking 'bout me like this. You done gone an' hurt my feelings. I oughtta keep what I brought over for myself.

REBA. What you done made now, Maybelle?

MAYBELLE. Nuttin'. It don't concern you. It's got my name on it now.

REBA. Come on. (*Tickles her.*) You ain't mad at your Reba now, are you?

MAYBELLE. (*Giving in, laughing out loud.*) Stop, stop Reba, you know I'm ticklish. Stop Reba.

REBA. (*Stops tickling her.*) I ain't got time to be carrying on like this. I got work to do. You pick some beans for me?

MAYBELLE. Yeah, but don't you want your surprise now?

REBA. (*Absentmindedly.*) What surprise?

MAYBELLE. Where's your mind Reba?

REBA. I don't know.

MAYBELLE. I told you I had got you something ... wait till you see what ...

REBA. *(Not really listening to her.)* Don't say nothing to Bailey but I had me one of those dreams again. My child was playing Maybelle, playing his horn, I declare he was, playing it like his life depended on it.

MAYBELLE. He's fine Reba. You would've heard if something was wrong. But wait ... wait till you see what I got. It'll cheer you right up. *(Takes out a big box, hands it to Reba.)* Voilà.

REBA. You didn't. I thought you brought something to eat. *(Stomps her feet.)* I know you didn't.

MAYBELLE. Well you know more than I know. Go 'head, open it up.

REBA. *(Excited like a child, goes through a ritual of balling her fists and stomping her feet, wanting to take the box, but holding back.)* I ... I can't. I can't. I just can't. I know you didn't get it. You didn't, did you? Well, did you? I just can't. I know what it is ... I told you I didn't need it. You did it, didn't you? You got it? I can't stand it. Naw, don't tell me ...

MAYBELLE. Half the joy of giving you a present Reba is watching you go through this stupid ass ritual. You ain't changed since you were five years old.

REBA. Oh shut up.

MAYBELLE. Go 'head, take the box.

REBA. Well, give it here. *(Takes the box.)* Maybelle, you shouldn't spend your money on me like this.

MAYBELLE. And miss this? *(Reba opens the box, it's a beautiful dress.)*

REBA. Oh Maybelle.

MAYBELLE. Yeah, it's the same one. Told you to buy it but you was too cheap. I had the girl put it on lay-a-way. Go on, slip it on. *(Reba takes off her housecoat and slips on the dress.)*

REBA. It's beautiful.

MAYBELLE. Lord, it was meant for you. That dressmaker knew what she was doing! Go look in the mirror. *(Reba looks in the mirror.)*

REBA. I'm ready. *(Sings.)* "Put on your red dress baby 'cause we going out tonight.... Put on your high heeled sneakers ..." *(Maybelle joins in, they sing and do an old-time dance with silly sequential steps. After a moment and unbeknownst to the two, Bailey and Dwayne enter. Bailey is carrying two suits in a cleaning bag, which he makes a big deal about hiding from Maybelle. They watch Maybelle and Reba a moment, enjoying the show.)*

MAYBELLE. Whew, I done worked up a sweat. That's my exercise for the day.

REBA. *(Kisses her.)* What would I do without you?

MAYBELLE. Well, I never plan for you to find out. *(Reba takes off the dress and slips back into her houscoat.)*

BAILEY. *(Gruffly, for he is always jealous witness when it comes to the intimacy between the two women.)* For once I'd like to walk through this door and not find you sittin' up in my house.

MAYBELLE. You know I brighten up your day Luke Bailey ... *(Maybelle takes out fingernail polish and an emery board, starts doing her nails.)*

REBA. *(Folding up the dress and putting it in the box.)* Bailey, call the Center. They called 'bout an hour ago.

DWAYNE. *(Overlapping, kissing her.)* Hi Aunt May.

MAYBELLE. Hi baby.

DWAYNE. Aunt May, you need me to cut the grass again this weekend?

MAYBELLE. Well, I don't know.

DWAYNE. How about trimming the hedges?

MAYBELLE. Boy, you sure is enterprising. *(Bailey is almost comical as he attempts to hide the suits from Maybelle while getting Reba to notice them.)*

BAILEY. *(To Reba.)* Which one?

DWAYNE. I'm going to see my Dad if he doesn't come home soon.

BAILEY. If your father wanted you to come, he'd send for you.

REBA. Bailey!

BAILEY. Well he would. Now Reba which ...

DWAYNE. Can I be excused?

REBA. *(Busying herself straightening up the house.)* Where you going?

DWAYNE.   Watch TV.

BAILEY.   *(Overlapping, whispering.)* Reba, which suit?

REBA.   You do your homework?

DWAYNE.   It's Saturday.

REBA.   What, you don't learn nothing except Monday through Friday?

BAILEY.   Boy, get it over with.

DWAYNE.   But, Daddy, I can do it tomorrow.

BAILEY.   Well, I was thinking that tomorrow a certain young man might want to go with his Daddy fishing.

DWAYNE.   *(Excited.)* Really?

BAILEY.   Yeah really, really. Reba which one? You know I got this thing coming up, you know, which suit?

REBA.   I don't know Bailey. You decide. *(To Dwayne.)* And Mister, you ain't going nowhere if I don't see you crack a book before the day is out. I mean that Dwayne. Maybelle, did you know that Bailey got nominated ...

BAILEY.   Reba.

REBA.   ... as volunteer of the year ...

BAILEY.   Reba don't ...

REBA.   ... down at the Boy's Club.

BAILEY.   Reba! Shit! *(Throws the suits on his chair, pouts.)* You getting to be just like her, can't keep nothing to yourself.

REBA.   Well it ain't no secret Bailey. He's got to give a speech.

MAYBELLE.   *(Crossing to Bailey.)* Well, that's good Bailey. That's why you been trying to hide them two suits looking silly? Ain't that one your funeral suit?

BAILEY.   Leave me alone.

MAYBELLE.   Wish that husband of mine would volunteer at something.

REBA.   He just enjoying his retirement.

MAYBELLE.   Wish he'd do it some other kinda way. All he wants to do is eat and sleep and pat on me, makes me sick. Let me get on out of here. Been up in here all day.

BAILEY.   Today ain't no different than any other. Don't know why you pretending you in a hurry now. Don't know

16

how you keep a husband ... 'cause if you was my wife....

MAYBELLE.   I wouldn't wish that on nobody. No offense Reba.

BAILEY.   Un-humm. Keep on talkin'.

MAYBELLE.   Bailey, I bet you didn't hear 'bout Thelma Butts? Heard tell her husband put her out on the corner ...

BAILEY.   *(Clearly interested.)* On the corner? Say what?!

MAYBELLE.   That's right. And she ain't passing out leaflets either. Passing out something else though.... And cheap!

REBA.   *(Overlapping, sharply.)* Maybelle, don't start that mess. I don't allow that kinda talk in my house, you know that. Need to stay out of other people's business, 'specially somebody nasty and trifling like that.

MAYBELLE.   *(Taken aback, sputtering.)* I was ... I ...

REBA.   I mean it.

BAILEY.   *(Conspiratorially to Maybelle.)* Tell me later.

REBA.   I heard that Bailey.

BAILEY.   Anybody else call?

REBA.   No, but I thought we'd hear from ... *(Catches herself.)*

BAILEY.   From who?

REBA.   Nothing.

BAILEY.   *(Annoyed.)* You on that again?

REBA.   On what Bailey?

BAILEY.   We ain't callin' him. Hear me? I mean that. If he got a dime to his name, Wendal can pick up the damn phone and call us ...

REBA.   Dwayne, what I tell you 'bout listening around grown folks talking? That's why you too grown now.

DWAYNE.   I wasn't listening.

BAILEY.   Boy, what your Grandma tell you? You better get them feet to marching. *(Dwayne exits.)*

REBA.   Wish you wouldn't talk about his father like that in front of him.

BAILEY.   Why not? Call a spade a spade, son or no son. His father is worthless. Playing in two-bit clubs, talking that funny talk.

REBA.   He's a musician and if he's happy ...

BAILEY.   Happy! How you know he's happy? He don't

bother to call here and tell you he's happy. *(To Maybelle.)* He rather play somewhere in a juke joint than make an honest living, he could've helped me down at the store ...

REBA. *(Angry.)* That store ain't everything Bailey.

BAILEY. It puts food on this table and in that boy's mouth upstairs. Ain't no damn music feedin' him ... ain't seen a horn blow no food this way ...

REBA. Hush Bailey, he'll hear you.

BAILEY. I don't give a damn. I don't want him growing up pretending that Wendal is something he's not ... making excuses for him all the time. You do that enough for everybody.

MAYBELLE. Well sir ... like I said I guess I better be getting on out of here ...

BAILEY. Hey, hey Maybelle, Reba tell you Junior coming home?

REBA. I forgot.

MAYBELLE. Really? Can't wait to see my boy.

BAILEY. Yeah, I'm gonna have him come down to the store and help me get those new shelves up. Think we gon' expand to that back room, start selling small appliances ...

REBA. He's only going to be here a few days Bailey. He's on leave, not work release.

BAILEY. Little hard work never hurt nobody and Junior, that boy, ain't never been scared of hard work. Not like Mr. Music man.

REBA. Crossing the line Bailey. I'm not in the mood today to be tangling with you about them boys.

BAILEY. Thirty years and you still don't see that boy for what he is. *(Exits in a huff.)*

REBA. I get so sick of him comparing Wendal to Junior.

MAYBELLE. Well Reba, honey, you know a man don't like softness in his sons.

REBA. Well, a man gets what he makes! *(Lights down on Bailey household and up on Wendal sitting on examination table.)*

WENDAL. Lord Jesus. God ... I ain't got no words. Just need a little favor. I know I'm in no position to bargain, but just let this one be different. I need it to be negative. So why don't you help me out here.... Oh shit. *(The Doctor enters and starts listening to his lungs. Nervous and with forced humor.)* It's just a little cough. You know, between you and me Doc, I don't believe that test was right, somebody in that lab must have screwed up. Should've had it redone, but me and the band was on the move. You know how that is. We don't stay in one place too long.

DOCTOR. How long have you been seropositive?

WENDAL. You mean when did I test?

DOCTOR. Yes.

WENDAL. About seven months ago. It wasn't here. I think it was in Florida. Don't know why I'm even here. You see I can't have AIDS. Look, I got a woman ... we thinking about getting married ...

DOCTOR. Any history of IV drug use?

WENDAL. What?

DOCTOR. I'm trying to ascertain Mr. Bailey if you have engaged in any risk behavior.

WENDAL. Smoke a little weed every now and then....

DOCTOR. So if I understand you correctly, you believe you contracted the virus through sexual intercourse?

WENDAL. No, you don't understand me correctly ...

DOCTOR. I know this is uncomfortable Mr. Bailey....

WENDAL. *(Putting on his shirt.)* All you doctors are alike. You my fourth one and every one of you trying to make me believe I'm dying.

DOCTOR. I didn't say anything about dying.... If you would just sit ...

WENDAL. You know this whole AIDS thing is some kind of conspiracy. Some more of ya'lls genocide.... Try and lay everything on us, cancer, drugs, whatever y'all think up. Well I'm here to tell you, y'alls AIDS better take a number, get in line. And you might as well wipe that silly grin off your face 'cause this is one nigger that ain't gon' lay down and die. Call it what you want, but I ain't sick. *(Yelling.)* You hear me? I'm fine ... *(Collapses with a coughing spell.)* I'm fine ...

DOCTOR. *(After a moment.)* Mr. Bailey, I think you and I both know that you are not fine ... now if we ...

WENDAL. Ya'll some cold mutherfuckers.

DOCTOR. Who do you think you're talking to?

WENDAL. All you had to do was tell us, didn't cost you nothing ... not a damn thing ...

DOCTOR. I'm not responsible for ...

WENDAL. Then who is? Now let me see if I got this right. You telling me I got bad blood ... well now ... remember ol' Tuskegee? I recall you told 'em they had bad blood too ... and then watched 'em rot to death. Ya'll got a history of this bad blood shit, don't you?

DOCTOR. Hey, hey time out. I tell you what, it's the end of the day ... the end of a very long day ... I've seen more patients today than most doctors see in a week so why don't you do us both a favor and cut the shit. You've seen four doctors, if you want I'll refer you to a fifth. I've been working in this epidemic for a long time and it's not because I have an affinity for your suffering or for that matter, my own. You understand? The bottom line: you screwed somebody, you didn't protect yourself, and that's your responsibility, not mine. Your partners will have to be notified. You can do it or you can have the State do it. Which will it be?

WENDAL. Just tell me how long I've been infected.

DOCTOR. I can't. Were any of your partners gay or bi-sexual men?

WENDAL. Naw. I don't mess with no men. *(Getting up, putting on his shirt.)* Time's up Doc, I gotta go.

DOCTOR. Wait. What about your girlfriend? I know it's difficult, but you have a responsibility to inform your partners. *(Loud.)* Mr. Bailey, you have a responsibility to inform your partners ... *(Repeats until Wendal phones home; he is using a public phone. It's a difficult conversation for him. Lights up on the Bailey household. He is practicing his speech. Phone rings, Bailey crosses to answer, carrying speech cards.)*

BAILEY. I'll get it. Hello. *(Wendal hesitates, is tempted to hang up.)* Hello?

WENDAL. Hello.

BAILEY. Speak up. I can hardly hear you. *(The following exchange is much talking at once and escalated voices as each tries to be heard.)*

WENDAL.   Hello. Hello Dad.

BAILEY.   Wendal?

REBA.   *(Crowding near the phone.)* Is that Wendal?

DWAYNE.   *(Overlapping on the upstairs extension.)* Daddy?

BAILEY.   *(Yelling in the phone.)* Boy, what are you doing up?

REBA.   He's a grown man Bailey.

BAILEY.   I'm talking about Dwayne. Dwayne's on that phone upstairs.

REBA.   He's supposed to be sleep.

WENDAL.   Dad, you still there?

BAILEY.   Yes. *(Phone.)* Wendal where are you?

DWAYNE.   Hi Daddy. How you doing?...

WENDAL.   Hey man, I thought you'd be sleep.

BAILEY.   He should be. Get off that phone Dwayne.

REBA.   Let the boy talk to his father.

DWAYNE.   I almost got enough money to come ... I wanna come see you.

REBA.   Is he ok? Is he coming?

WENDAL.   I may be coming there. Dad, you still there?

BAILEY.   *(To Reba, irritated.)* Yes. Yes.

REBA.   *(Whispers to Bailey.)* Be nice. Try to get along.

BAILEY.   *(In phone.)* Wendal? *(Irritated, quickly before interrupted again.)* I'm here, got this dinner to go to, got to give a speech ... getting honored ... volunteer of the year ... all the boys voted for me ... role model ...

REBA.   Bailey, you ain't got to shout, he ain't hard of hearing. Let me talk.

BAILEY.   And Dwayne and I going fishing.

DWAYNE.   I'm getting straight As, except for a few Cs and couple of Bs.

BAILEY.   I can't hear myself think. DWAYNE GET OFF THAT PHONE NOW.

WENDAL.   *(Overlapping.)* I want you to know that I love you Dwayne.

BAILEY.   Didn't I tell you to hang up? It's past his bedtime. HANG THAT PHONE UP DWAYNE. *(Dwayne hangs up.)*

WENDEL.   *(Overlapping.)* Did you hear me Dwayne?

REBA.   Let me talk Bailey.

21

BAILEY. Just a minute. Well, you sound good. Your brother coming home.

WENDAL. I was thinking about coming home ... I'd like to see you ... Dad I....

BAILEY. *(Overlapping.)* Coming home a sergeant. Service made a man of him. I always did say that boy was gonna 'mount to something.

WENDEL. Yeah, you always did. Dad ...

BAILEY. Yeah, I'm real proud of him. You don't sound right. You in some kind of trouble?

WENDAL. Why do you always ask me that? Why do I always have to be in some kind of trouble to call home.

BAILEY. So you not in trouble. You working?

WENDAL. Yeah. We're trying to get a record deal. Looks like it might come through. Supposed to have a meeting with this producer ...

BAILEY. *(Obviously disgusted.)* Your mother is here. She's right here. Let me let you talk to her.

WENDAL. Dad wait.

BAILEY. *(Overlapping.)* Wait. Wait just a moment. Here she is. *(Hands the phone to Reba, clearly exasperated, exits.)*

REBA. Before you say a word, Mama's gon' tell you what's waiting on you. Fried corn, candied yams. Your mouth watering? Chicken and dressing, greens that'll make you shout, beef so tender the butcher wanna buy it back. Then we gon' finish it all off with some 7-Up pound cake and Neapolitan ice cream, trim it with Maybelle's sweet potato pie.

WENDAL. Have mercy!

REBA. You just say when. I'm a get that guest room dolled up for Simone. Dwayne done moved most of your stuff from the attic in his room so you can probably bunk in with him.... Lord, the house is gon' be full again.... I can't wait. Simone cooking any better?

WENDAL. *(Wendal starts coughing uncontrollably.)* I gotta go. Talk to you later Mama. *(He hangs up, she exits. Lights to Douglass and Simone area. Douglass is sitting at a desk. Simone enters singing. She has just bathed and is wearing Wendal's robe. She surveys the house with pleasure, maybe puffing up the pillows, straightening things for the umpteenth time. Wendal watches both of them for a minute, clearly debating to whom he should approach first. The following scene should be paced so that the dialogue and action overlap. Wendal's world is literally split between the two relationships.)*

DOUGLASS.   How did you get in?

WENDAL.   The door was open. I saw her leave.

DOUGLASS.   I thought we agreed ...

SIMONE.   Finally! What do you think? Pretty proud of myself. What do you think about the color? I got this serious vision about wallpapering the whole place.

DOUGLASS.   Wendal, did you hear me? We've been through this before. I thought we agreed ...

WENDAL.   This couldn't wait. *(Kissing him, holds on.)*

DOUGLASS.   Well, I'm glad to see you too.

SIMONE.   How 'bout a kiss? Lay one on me. *(She kisses Wendal.)*

SIMONE and DOUGLASS.   You ok?

WENDAL.   Yeah. You smell good.

DOUGLASS.   Yeah, I thought I'd try a new scent.

SIMONE.   Just got out the shower. Boy, where did you get that cologne? I like it.

DOUGLASS.   I went by the club last night. Where were you?

WENDAL.   Somebody was supposed to sit in for me. I went away for a few days. Needed to think.

SIMONE.   How come you didn't call?

WENDAL.   We got through late every night. I thought you'd be studying.

SIMONE.   How considerate. *(Hands Wendal the lotion. Wendal kneels and starts applying the lotion and massaging her feet.)* I thought we could fix up a spare room for Dwayne when he comes to visit.... Hello in there, a spare room for Dwayne, your son....

DOUGLASS.   What's her name go with you?

WENDAL.   You know her name.

SIMONE.   I may have some good news. A teacher is leaving. They're going to recommend me to replace her. My own classroom! Isn't that great?

WENDAL.   How long is she gon' be gone?

DOUGLASS. I don't know.

SIMONE. It's a big class, but I'll have an aide.

WENDAL. Where's the kids?

DOUGLASS. She let them go to some concert that I suspect will give them permanent hearing damage.

SIMONE. Of course I might not get it. But think positive, that's what you're always telling me ... *(She moans with pleasure.)* That feels good. Nobody has hands like you.

DOUGLASS. I just found out today that Alison needs braces. At her age! I told Beth maybe we should try a pair of pliers ...

WENDAL. Pliers! That's cold blooded Douglass. *(Douglass laughs; Simone laughs at the same time.)* What? What is it?

DOUGLASS. You're right.

WENDAL. I have something to tell you.

SIMONE. *(Overlapping.)* Oh, just that the kids were teasing me about you today. You were a big hit with them. You should see them strutting around, they all think they're sax players now ... and of course the girls all want to grow up and marry you. *(Simone laughs again, is bubbling over with excitement.)*

DOUGLASS. Beth is taking the kids to see her mother. I'll be a free man for a week, one whole glorious week with no demands.

WENDAL. I have something to tell you. There's something else. Come on Simone, what's up?

DOUGLASS. I have to see a few clients in the morning. Why people wait to the last minute to file.... You could tell *Simone* you had a gig.... Thought maybe we could go somewhere ...

WENDAL. Will you shut up for a minute?

DOUGLASS. What did I say?

SIMONE. Touchy. Touchy.

WENDAL. Nothing ... I just ...

DOUGLASS. Let me fix you a drink.

WENDAL. How about a beer?

DOUGLASS and SIMONE. *(Both exit to get a beer.)* Ok.

WENDAL. But I can get it.

SIMONE.   That's ok.

DOUGLASS.   *(Off.)* You want something to eat? You've lost weight.

SIMONE.   *(Off.)* Dwayne called but it was a strange message. He said your father said to call your mother but not to tell your mother ... something like that. You see the doctor before you left on Friday? Did they find out what's wrong with you?

DOUGLASS.   I cooked. The roast would melt in your mouth.

SIMONE.   I tried a new recipe, but I took pity on you and threw it out.

DOUGLASS.   You sure I can't tempt you?

WENDAL.   *(Irritated.)* No.

DOUGLASS.   *(Entering, hands him a beer.)* It was just a simple question?

SIMONE.   *(Entering.)* No?

WENDAL.   They want to run some more tests.

SIMONE.   Sorry, we're out of beer.

WENDAL.   That's ok.

SIMONE.   More tests?

WENDAL.   What's with the silent treatment? You know how I feel about her. And you're the one that said it was just a good time.... And for seven years, we've been having a real swell time, haven't we?... You ever get the seven year itch Douglass?

SIMONE.   You telling me everything?

WENDAL.   *(Sharply.)* You think I'm lying?

SIMONE.   Is that a challenge or an answer?

WENDAL.   No.

DOUGLASS.   You could have spared me this dark mood you're in.... Why don't you take it on home to Simone.

SIMONE.   *(Snuggling.)* I'm glad you're home. I missed you.

WENDAL.   I needed to talk to you.

DOUGLASS.   My back's been bothering me again. Will you do my shoulders? *(Wendal massages his shoulders.)*

WENDAL.   How's that?

DOUGLASS.   Good. You really ought to go in business. *(Douglass moans with pleasure.)*

WENDAL. You wanna hear a joke?

SIMONE. My sister may stay with us for a few days. That husband of hers is acting up again.

DOUGLASS. Not particularly.

WENDAL. What's the difference between a black man and a fag.

DOUGLASS. I can hardly wait for this punch line.

SIMONE. I don't know why she doesn't leave him. I keep telling her she can do better.

WENDAL. One doesn't have to tell his mother. *(Laughs, seeing Douglass didn't get it.)* You don't get it?

SIMONE. I have another surprise for you. *(Dramatically opens her robe, revealing a sexy nightgown.)* Voilà! *(In a Dracula voice, she parades around him.)* I want to make love to you my sweet.

WENDAL. Be still my heart.

DOUGLASS. Wendal?

SIMONE. *(In the same Dracula voice.)* Your heart can be still, but I was hoping something else would get to moving. *(Continues to parade around and tease him.)*

WENDAL. What am I going to do with you?

DOUGLASS. Now can we talk about something else? I can make reservations ...

SIMONE. I can think of something my sweet.

WENDAL. See, my mother is not the only one I have to tell. I'm trying to tell you....

DOUGLASS. Tell me what Wendal?

SIMONE. Tell me.

WENDAL. What?

SIMONE. Go 'head tell me. When were you planning to ask me? The answer is yes, yes, yes, yes.

WENDAL. I don't think we should see each other anymore. At least ... not like ... you know what I mean ...

DOUGLASS. No, I don't know what you mean.

SIMONE. I found it. You know....

WENDAL. Don't be dense.

DOUGLASS. Well, talk English.

SIMONE. I wasn't snooping, not exactly. I was just straightening out your night stand and I just happened across....

DOUGLASS. *(Pause.)* I knew this day was coming. Trust you to be creative in breaking the news. Fag jokes, no less. So, you decided to marry her, huh?

SIMONE. It's a tad expensive, but I'm sure it's really beautiful. *(Hugs him.)* I love you so much. All weekend I've been on cloud nine. When were you going to ask me?

WENDAL. Marry? I got AIDS Douglass.

SIMONE. When?

WENDAL. Well, this certainly wasn't what I had in mind.

DOUGLASS. Where did I put that brochure?

WENDAL. I can't believe you went rummaging through my things.

DOUGLASS. I figured we could go to that same place ... maybe even get the same room.... Now, where did I put it?

WENDAL. What?

SIMONE. I wasn't rummaging ... I was looking for a number ... this ring, it's on lay-a-way for me, isn't it?

WENDAL. Who else?

DOUGLASS. *(Looking, somewhat frantically for the brochure.)* Remember how we jumped on that bed so it would look like you slept in it....

WENDAL. We broke it. But Douglass what's that got to do ...

SIMONE. I know it was supposed to be a surprise. If you want, I'll be surprised again ... over and over again....

DOUGLASS. I felt like a kid again. The maid, what was her name again?

WENDAL. Why do you always have to push?

SIMONE. *(Annoyed.)* 'Cause somebody needs to jump-start your ass.

DOUGLASS. What was her name?

WENDAL. I don't know Douglass ... I'm really not in a mood for a trip down memory lane.... Didn't you hear what I said? I tested positive ...

SIMONE. You're right, maybe I am pushing. I just don't understand this. What's happening to us Wendal?

DOUGLASS. She was a doll. I think she knew. I'm sure she knew. Two black men traveling alone together ...

27

SIMONE. I live with you. I sleep with you. I used to make love with you, at least until you started shutting me out.

DOUGLASS. "You boys sure know how to mess up a room. Look like you been riding the devil in here."

SIMONE. I moved in here because that's what you said you wanted ...

WENDAL. Douglass ...

DOUGLASS. Jasmine. That was her name. Jasmine.

WENDAL. It was what you wanted.

SIMONE. I thought it was what we both wanted. I've tried not to push, tried like hell but you always knew I wanted more ... I never made that a secret ... I have no desire to be somebody's trial wife or trial roommate or trial nothing ... understand? It's either shit or get off the pot baby.

DOUGLASS. *(Finding the brochure, crosses to Wendal with it.)* Here it is. I found it.

WENDAL. I can't. I'm sorry ...

SIMONE. I'm sure there's some humor in this somewhere.

WENDAL. This virus is kicking my ass Douglass ... I guess it's a test of my faith ... I know death is a part of life ...

SIMONE. Can't you at least be a little more original? You're sorry. That's all you can say is you're sorry.

DOUGLASS. When'd you find out?

WENDAL. A couple days ago.

SIMONE. I don't believe you. Why did you buy the ring in the first place?

DOUGLASS. And you're just now telling me?

WENDAL. You have to believe me. I wanted things to work. I love you. I wanted you to be my wife. With you I thought I had a future.

DOUGLASS. I don't believe you.

SIMONE. Past tense?

WENDAL. No. But you're the one who set the rules, way in the beginning. No strings, no commitment.

SIMONE. I want a commitment.

WENDAL. Me too. But everything has changed.

DOUGLASS. This can't be happening.

WENDAL. I knew I had to tell you and I'm still trying to

find the right words to tell Simone ...

DOUGLASS.   Well, you didn't seem to have any problem finding the right words to tell me ...

SIMONE.   Prove it.

WENDAL.   She has no idea.

SIMONE.   I said prove it. Make love to me.

WENDAL.   I'm scared, real scared Douglass.

SIMONE.   I need you.

WENDAL.   I need you too. (*Simone starts to undress him. Douglass slowly tears the brochure into little pieces.*)

DOUGLASS.   You know I'm not sick. I've been gaining weight. Just this morning Beth told me I was getting fat.

WENDAL.   I can't do that to you.

DOUGLASS.   You think I gave you this shit, don't you?

WENDAL.   I just want to settle down.

DOUGLASS.   You think it was me?

SIMONE.   You are my best friend.

WENDAL.   You know you're my best friend.

DOUGLASS.   Don't use that word. I am your lover!

WENDAL.   I need a friend.

DOUGLASS.   And I didn't give it to you.

WENDAL.   Right now Douglass that's the least of my worries. It really doesn't matter ...

SIMONE.   I'm not letting go.

DOUGLASS.   It most certainly does matter.

SIMONE.   I can't let go. Hold me Wendal.

WENDAL.   Simone, baby don't. I can't. (*Wendal and Simone kiss deeply.*)

DOUGLASS.   I trusted you.

WENDAL.   God, give me strength. I'm ... so scared....

DOUGLASS.   I trusted you.

WENDAL.   That goes both ways.

DOUGLASS.   I'm the one with the family ...

SIMONE.   I want to be your family. (*He struggles, they struggle, but ultimately need and passion win out. Wendal and Simone lie back on the bed or floor.*)

DOUGLASS.   We were careful ... (*Softer to himself.*) we were, weren't we Wendal? (*Lights shift to Simone and Wendal in bed.*)

whole pharmacy?

NURSE. I'll be back in a few minutes with your wheelchair.

WENDAL. Not necessary.

NURSE. Hospital rules. *(She exits.)*

DOUGLASS. I don't know why you insist on boarding a train today. You sure this trip is ok with your doctor?

WENDAL. Yes Douglass.

DOUGLASS. I wish you wouldn't go until you're feeling stronger.

WENDAL. I'm going Douglass.

DOUGLASS. I can get you a hotel room for a few days ...

WENDAL. Douglass I'm going. I can't wait. Few home cooked meals, my family, be good as new.

DOUGLASS. Maybe you're expecting too much Wendal.

WENDAL. I have to.

DOUGLASS. Just don't want to see you hurt ... *(Wendal laughs.)* What's so funny?

WENDAL. AIDS done already hurt my feelings Douglass. I don't know how much more hurt I can get. *(Pause.)* Appreciate you taking care of things ... figure you ain't such a bad guy, outside of my family, you the longest relationship I've had ... that oughtta count for something ... *(Hugs him.)*

DOUGLASS. Hey, I hope you aren't getting sentimental on me. I'm trying my damnest to be butch here. *(They both laugh, a moment while they grapple with the loss.)* And look at you, you got your shirt buttoned all wrong. *(Re-buttons his shirt.)*

WENDAL. Thought it looked funny. You know, you'd make somebody a good husband.

DOUGLASS. Real cute. *(Finishing the buttoning.)* There. *(Pause.)* I may never see you again.

WENDAL. Don't.

DOUGLASS. Don't what?

WENDAL. Come on let's get out of here. I don't need a wheelchair. *(Wendal picks up the suitcase.)*

DOUGLASS. Don't try to lift that. I can get it.

WENDAL. I can get it.

DOUGLASS. I said I would get it.

WENDAL. I'm not helpless Douglass.

DOUGLASS.   *(They struggle.)* Would you let me carry the damn suitcase?!!!

WENDAL.   Yeah, I'll let you carry it and I love you too. *(A moment as they both struggle with the loss, regrouping, teasing.)* Just psyching you out. Carry the damn thing so I can strut out of here looking like my old fine cute self. Who knows, somebody may look my way, give me a little play ...

DOUGLASS.   *(Laughing with him.)* Nigger please, not hardly ...

NURSE.   *(Rolling the wheelchair.)* Time to go home Mr. Bailey.

DOUGLASS.   *(Helping Wendal in the chair.)* That's right Mr. Bailey, time for you to go home. *(They exit.)*

END OF ACT ONE

ACT TWO

Lights up on Bailey household.

Wendal, Junior and Dwayne are in the kitchen preparing dinner. Reba, Maybelle and Bailey are in the living room; Reba is dressed in her gifts, the red dress, the bracelet.

REBA.   I feel so useless. You all don't need any help in there?

DWAYNE, WENDAL and JUNIOR.   *(Off, in unison.)* No.

WENDAL.   *(Off.)* That's the third time Mama.

MAYBELLE.   It sure is good to have them home. And they got the place looking so good.

REBA.   They got most of the upstairs painted and they supposed to paint in here before Junior leave out.

BAILEY.   *(Mumbling.)* I still got them cabinets down at the store I want done.

MAYBELLE.   *(Overlapping.)* Wendal helping out too?

REBA.   Oh yeah.

MAYBELLE.   He don't look too well to me.

REBA.   Trying to fatten him up a little.

BAILEY.   He look OK. Don't you all start borrowing trouble with all that fussing over him. *(Dwayne enters, starts setting the table.)*

MAYBELLE.   *(To Dwayne.)* How's it going in there? *(To Reba and Bailey.)* Whatever they cooking, I hope we gon' be able to eat it. *(To Dwayne.)* Honey, do it look edible?

DWAYNE.   I don't know. It look OK.

BAILEY.   Junior's a pretty good cook. It's Wendal ain't never learned his way 'round a kitchen.

REBA.   Father like son.

MAYBELLE.   *(Laughs.)* You got that right. She got you there Bailey.

BAILEY.   I can cook. Reba know I can cook, she just don't

41

let me.

REBA.   Bailey please.   *(Dwayne moves Maybelle's purse on the floor, Maybelle screeches.)*

MAYBELLE.   Un-Un. Un-Un child. Don't put my purse on that floor. That's bad luck. Put a woman's purse on the floor and she'll never have any money.

DWAYNE.   Sorry.

MAYBELLE.   Just hand it here. *(Dwayne hands her her purse.)*

BAILEY.   I don't know why you clutching that purse so, you know you ain't got nothing but a dollar in it. All your money if you got any is up between them bosoms.

REBA.   Bailey!

BAILEY.   Why you Baileying me. I ain't never seen Maybelle pull money from no purse. Maybelle need money she going between them pillows up there.

MAYBELLE.   I got my money where I know it's safe. You just jealous. Some fool steal your wallet, you's a man without a dime. Somebody steal my purse, *(Cups her breasts.)* I'm still loaded.

REBA.   *(Laughs out loud.)* Now that's the truth.

MAYBELLE.   And you oughtta be complimenting your wife on how nice she looks instead of worrying 'bout where I put my money. She look real sexy in that dress, don't she?

BAILEY.   Little flashy, I think, for Reba.

WENDAL.   *(Enters, has overheard the last comment.)* I think she looks beautiful, real special tonight.

REBA.   Well thank you son.

BAILEY.   *(Defensive.)* I didn't say she didn't look beautiful. *(To Reba.)* That bracelet Junior bought you, now it look nice with that dress. *(To Wendal.)* Did you see the bracelet your brother bought your Mama?

WENDAL.   No. *(Admires the bracelet.)* That's nice.

BAILEY.   And he got me this watch. Did I show it you? It's got a real diamond.

WENDAL.   Yeah. You showed it to me when I first got home.

BAILEY.   And he got Dwayne a little jacket. Did you show your father your jacket Dwayne?

REBA. He can show him later Bailey.

BAILEY. Oh. OK. That's fine with me. Junior just bought us home such nice things ... I just thought Wendal might like to see 'em.

DWAYNE. Daddy's buying me some skates.

BAILEY. I don't know nothing 'bout that.

WENDEL. *(His arm around Dwayne.)* That's because I'm buying 'em.

BAILEY. Oh.

JUNIOR. *(Enters with a big fork and spatula, deadpan serious.)* We got a fire extinguisher?

REBA. What?

MAYBELLE. Lord. Lord. I knew I should have eaten before I left home.

JUNIOR. Wendal kinda set fire to the chicken.

WENDEL. *(Laughing.)* Quit lying on me man. *(Bailey realizes Junior's kidding, starts to laugh.)*

JUNIOR. *(Laughing out hilariously.)* And the potatoes ...

BAILEY. I ain't surprised.

WENDAL. Man stop ...

JUNIOR. And the pot holder ... the kitchen curtains ...

WENDAL. He's lying Mama. He's lying ...

REBA. *(Getting up, on her way to the kitchen.)* What have you all done to my kitchen?

JUNIOR. *(Stopping her.)* I'm kidding. I'm kidding. Everything's cool.

REBA. Get out of my way Junior. I don't know what made me take leave of my senses, letting ya'll cook.

JUNIOR. Come on Mama. I'm kidding. The kitchen still in one piece. This your party, you shouldn't have to cook. All you supposed to do is sit right down here and enjoy this masterpiece or burnt pieces your two sons and grandson have concocted. Wendal's specialty this evening is A'LA crisp.

WENDAL. OK man.

MAYBELLE. That's OK. Wendal's a star. He ain't meant to do common labor, ain't that right baby? *(Kisses him.)*

WENDAL. Yeah. That's right. Thank you Aunt May.

BAILEY and JUNIOR. Shit.

43

MAYBELLE. So, what's the entertainment this evening? I know you and Junior gon 'sing.

JUNIOR. Well ...

REBA. Maybe you can play something on your horn for us.

BAILEY. That horn'll wake up the whole neighborhood this time of night ...

MAYBELLE. Ya'll come on and sing a song, sing the song that used to make me wanna holler. Ya'll gon' do that for your Auntie May?

WENDAL. Well, I don't know. My throat's been bothering me.

BAILEY. I thought that's how you made your living boy. How you gon' work playing music when you complaining about your throat bothering you?

REBA. Ya'll sing a little bit. It would do me good to hear ya'll sing together.

MAYBELLE. It'll do me good too.

JUNIOR. Ok. How 'bout it man?

WENDAL. Ok.

JUNIOR. What's the song Auntie May?

WENDAL. Start us off.

MAYBELLE. Ok, I'll help you out. *(Maybelle starts humming a blues song such as "Kiddeo."* Wendal joins in and takes the lead. Junior accompanies, then everybody joins in. Bailey gets up and starts dancing a wild exaggerated dance, maybe the funky chicken.)*

REBA. Go on Bailey. Go on now ...

BAILEY. Come on Maybelle. Come on here.

MAYBELLE. *(Getting up and dancing with him.)* What are you doing Luke Bailey? You better sit down before I embarrass you. You know you can't keep up with a young woman like me. Come on and dance with me Junior.

BAILEY. *(Dancing with Dwayne.)* Come on boy. *(Wendal dances with his mother; clearly everybody is enjoying themselves; Maybelle becomes winded from Junior spinning her around, sits down exhausted.)*

44

MAYBELLE.   Oh Lordy ... ooh ...

BAILEY.   What's wrong Maybelle, you can't keep up with the old man? I thought you was gon' embarrass somebody this evening.

MAYBELLE.   I know when to stop making a fool of myself, something you oughtta learn Luke Bailey. You know you ain't gon' be able to move in the morning.

JUNIOR.   I ain't sang that in years.

MAYBELLE.   It still sound good.

JUNIOR.   *(To Wendal.)* Man, I see you ain't lost your touch. Still know how to croon.

BAILEY.   Yeah, sound pretty good if I say so myself.

WENDAL.   *(Surprised, pleasantly.)* Thanks Dad.

BAILEY.   Yeah, sound damn good. Never said you didn't have a voice. You know we having this program down at the Center on the twenty-first. Maybe you can sing at it. People down there always asking me 'bout you, wanting to know when you gon' make a record, you know how people are, wanna make you out more than you is. You don't have to answer me now, just think about it.... They may have me do another speech ... I told you 'bout my speech ...

JUNIOR.   Man you been telling us 'bout that speech ...

MAYBELLE.   Yes Jesus!

WENDAL.   *(Seeing that Bailey looks a little hurt.)* I'd like to hear you speak Dad. Never heard you before an audience. It can be tricky.

BAILEY.   You got that right.

WENDAL.   Let me know what you want me to sing.

JUNIOR.   Well, what about me? Maybe I can do a little background. *(Starts doing some rifts; clearly carrying a tune is not Junior's strong point.)* Do wah do wha ...

BAILEY.   *(Cutting him off.)* I want you to do a solo, it ain't gon' be but a few minutes ...

REBA.   *(Noticing how much Wendal is sweating.)* Wendal, you ok?

BAILEY.   He's fine. Now Wendal ...

WENDAL.   *(Overlapping.)* Fine Mama, just need a little water. Better change my shirt too. Be right back. *(He exits.)*

MAYBELLE. Oh Lord, look now how this knee done swole ...

BAILEY. That knee ain't swole, that's just fat Maybelle! *(Falls out laughing.)*

JUNIOR. *(Trying to conceal his laughter.)* Nothing like a woman with a little flesh on her bones, though, ain't that right Auntie May?

MAYBELLE. That's right and I wanna thank you Junior. Your father eyesight just failing him. And you know what they say ... every time a fat woman shakes, a skinny woman looses her home.

REBA. Please, don't you two get started.

MAYBELLE. I ain't getting nothing started. I feel too good this evening. My boys are home.

BAILEY. They's mens Maybelle, face it. You getting old.

MAYBELLE. They'll always be my boys. I don't make no difference between them and my own four.

WENDAL. *(Enters, he has changed his shirt.)* How they doing?

MAYBELLE. Got 'em all married off. They they wives' problems now. Speaking of wives, you and that child looking to get hooked up? What's her name again?

WENDAL. Simone.

MAYBELLE. Yeah. Pretty black thang.

WENDAL. *(A little uncomfortable.)* Well right now she's back there and I'm here. I just wanted to come home for a while. Didn't realize how much I missed everybody.

REBA. Well we missed you too. Didn't we Bailey?

BAILEY. Yeah, I'm glad he's here. Now that you sleeping through the night again maybe I can finally get some decent shut-eye.

MAYBELLE. Yeah Wendal having you home does this house good. This place needed livening up. All Auntie May need now is a little sustenance. Junior, ain't there no cheese slices or bread sticks? Ain't seen no dinner party without no hor-de-derves.

WENDAL. Won't be long. *(Exits to the kitchen.)*

BAILEY. *(Overlapping.)* Maybelle, you can't even pronounce the word.

MAYBELLE.   Aw shut up Bailey.

JUNIOR.   *(Overlapping.)* You have to talk to Wendal. This his thang, I'm just following orders.

WENDAL.   *(Enters with fancy folded napkins which he places on the table.)* Everything's almost ready. We'll seat you now. *(With much formality, Wendal seats his mother at the table, Junior seats Maybelle while Dwayne attempts to seat Bailey.)*

BAILEY.   *(To Dwayne.)* I can manage my chair on my own, thank you.

WENDEL.   *(Switches the forks around.)* Table looks nice Dwayne.

MAYBELLE.   Where you learn how to do all this?

WENDAL.   I've done my share of waiting tables. First course: shrimp cocktail. *(Snaps his finger in the air for Junior and Dwayne to follow him.)* Gentlemen, if you please ...

JUNIOR.   *(Grumbling good naturedly as he exits.)* Now Mr. Head Waiter, I didn't know you snapping your fingers at me was part of the deal. I don't see why we can't eat buffet style, should've set up a soup kitchen ... *(Dwayne and Junior exit behind Wendal.)*

MAYBELLE.   *(Shaking her head.)* Umph, that's not a good sign. Whenever the service is too fancy, the food ain't worth shit. I bet we gon' get one shrimp.

BAILEY.   You lucky to have that. Now you eat everything else and you gon' eat what these boys done cooked with a smile on your face. Ain't that right?

MAYBELLE.   Yes sir massa.

BAILEY.   Think it's kinda nice they giving their Mama a break.

REBA.   That's more life I've seen in Wendal since he been here. And I love to hear my boy sing.

BAILEY.   Yeah. Kinda put me in mind of the old days. Every Saturday, remember how he used to put on them little shows for us...?

REBA.   Yeah.

MAYBELLE.   And that sorry James Brown act ya'll used to do. I used to have to drag my boys over here so ya'll would have a little audience.

47

REBA. Honey, yeah, Bailey and that cape.

MAYBELLE. Wendal falling down to the ground squealing like a pig and there come Bailey trying to get on the good foot with that toilet paper roll.... 'Member that Bailey? How you'd drape Wendal? When you was younger you used to have a lot more spirit.

BAILEY. I still do. *(Getting excited.)* Maybe after dinner I'll see if Wendal still remember our little routine we used to do ...

MAYBELLE. Oh Lord we gon' be subjected to that again. *(Reba suddenly reaches over and kisses Bailey.)*

BAILEY. What's that for?

REBA. Nothing. I'm just so damn happy.

MAYBELLE. Reba, honey, did you say damn?

REBA. Yes. Damn. Damn. Damn. Damn happy!

JUNIOR. *(Enters carrying a covered platter, sets it down in the middle of the table.)* Un Un Un. Don't touch. Wendal says no unveiling till he's present. Forgot how bossy he is. Been leading me around all day, shopping and practicing ... made me read every label, on every can, on every aisle ... took us three hours ... three hours in somebody's grocery store ... I'm 'bout to fall out and he's whistling Dixie ...

WENDAL. *(Off.)* Junior. Hey bro' ...

JUNIOR. See? I got to get on back to the Army so I can get me some rest. *(He exits.)*

MAYBELLE. That boy know he love his brother. *(Reaches for the cover of the platter.)* Shoot. I need to prepare my stomach.

BAILEY. *(Smacks her hands.)* Wendal wants us to wait so we gon' wait. *(Wendal brings in another dish.)* Everything smells good son.

WENDAL. Hope it tastes good. I don't know if Junior read the recipes right. *(He exits.)*

MAYBELLE. Umph! Did you hear that? They got to read while they cook. Lord, maybe I got a candy bar in my purse.

BAILEY. *(Laughing.)* I ain't got a candy bar but I got some peanuts in the basement. *(They all crack up laughing.)*

WENDAL. *(Enters.)* What's so funny?

MAYBELLE and REBA. Nothing.

BAILEY. *(Overlapping.)* Nothing son. Nothing. Just enjoying ourselves in here. *(Dwayne comes out carrying a pot with sauce dripping, he's soiled the front of his shirt. Wendal is behind him carrying a casserole dish.)*

REBA. Dwayne you done spilled something on your shirt.

DWAYNE. Oh.

MAYBELLE. You have to be careful. Watch what you doing.

BAILEY. Leave the boy alone, it'll wash out.

WENDAL. I'll get him something.

REBA. Maybe you should've cooked in some old clothes.

JUNIOR. *(Enters with another dish.)* Last one. Ready to dig in?

WENDAL. *(Enters with an apron, a frilly type.)* No, remember, we're serving 'em.

MAYBELLE. We getting served? Well can I make me a special order?

REBA. Maybelle.

WENDAL. Here Dwayne. Put on Mama's apron while you serve. *(Ties apron around Dwayne.)* There.

BAILEY. Now he looks like a little sissy faggot. *(Junior laughs loud, everybody snickers except Wendal whose whole demeanor has changed.)*

REBA. I think he looks kinda cute.

WENDAL. I don't see anything funny.

DWAYNE. *(With much disdain.)* I don't look like no fag. *(Takes the apron off.)*

WENDAL. *(Trying to control his rage.)* What you say? *(Dwayne looks scared, knows his father is angry, is confused and embarrassed. Grabbing him.)* Answer me. I said what did you say?

DWAYNE. *(Slightly indignant.)* I said I didn't look like no fag.

WENDAL. I don't ever want to hear you say something like that again. You understand me?

BAILEY. I don't know why you jumping all over the boy. They call theyselves that.

WENDAL. So! We call ourselves nigger, but that don't mean we are one. You don't allow him to use that word in this house. Do you? Go on Dwayne say nigger to your grandfather. Say nigger like you said fag.... Go on, say it ...

BAILEY. Dwayne you bet not say one word ...

49

WENDAL.   Why the silence now? Dwayne, I told you ...

REBA.   I'd like to talk about something else, like this dinner ...

JUNIOR.   Yeah man, I don't know why you all upset, ain't nobody called you a fag. It was just a joke.

MAYBELLE.   I sure am ready to eat this food.

WENDAL.   *(Overlapping.)* You'll never change. I guess it's just a joke you raising him like you tried to do me ... with the same small minded ...

BAILEY.   At least I'm raising him.

WENDAL.   Is that what you call it?

REBA.   Wendal!

JUNIOR.   Whoa! You need to back up man. *(Junior sits at the table.)* Come on. Everybody let's eat.

BAILEY.   *(Angry.)* I don't know why in the Sam hell you come home. You ain't satisfied unless you upsetting everybody. Gotta defy me no matter what. Thank God I got me one son that's got some sense, but you, you wanna ram that crazy shit down my damn throat every time I turn around, well who needs it? This is my house ... you hear me? Mine. And the door swings both ways. If you don't like it Mister, then let the door hit you where the good Lord split you. You can take your narrow ass back where....

REBA.   Bailey! That's enough.

DWAYNE.   I'm sorry Dad. I didn't mean to make you mad.

WENDAL.   I'm not mad at you Dwayne.

DWAYNE.   You not getting ready to leave again, are you?

REBA.   No. Your Dad is gon' be right here. Now everybody let's eat. We letting the food get cold. *(Puts on the apron, starts serving, in silence everybody passes food.)* Dwayne sit down. *(Dwayne hesitates, looks at his father expectantly.)* I said sit down Dwayne. *(Dwayne takes his seat at the table.)* What part of the chicken you want Bailey?

BAILEY.   *(Still angry.)* I don't care.

JUNIOR.   Old man, you better care. Me and Wendal went through a lot of trouble. Ain't that right Bro? Wendal had me inspecting every chicken in the store.

MAYBELLE.   Wendal, baby you and Junior done cooked a

feast here. Yes Lord! I may have to hurt myself.

REBA. *(Looks up at Wendal who's still standing away from the table.)* Wendal?

WENDAL. *(Looks at all of them for a moment, hesitates.)* Sorry Mama. I think I lost my appetite. *(Wendal exits. Lights. Later on that night. Wendal comes downstairs. He's sick. With much effort, he moves to the kitchen and gets ice water from the refrigerator. Takes his medicine, moves back to the living room. Reba enters wearing a robe. Wendal quickly hides the medicine.)*

REBA. I didn't know anyone was down here. You feeling any better?

WENDAL. A little.

REBA. How 'bout some ginger ale? I don't know why, I just woke up and had a taste for some pop. You want some?

WENDAL. No.

REBA. Sorry everything didn't work out like you planned this evening. *(Pause.)* Everything was going fine. Why'd you have to fight with him?

WENDAL. *(Moving to the couch.)* Why don't you ask him that question?

REBA. *(Walking around the room.)* I'm glad you and Junior gon' paint in here. I'm a help. Since you all been here I feel kinda useful again. Lately, I seem to have a lot of time on my hands. Sometimes I catch myself sitting all day right there on that couch and Lord this house can get so quiet. With Dwayne not needing me as much ... don't get me wrong, I'm not complaining. He's got a mind of his own, just like you did. Scares your father. Sometimes a father can't see his son for his own failings. You ever think about that?

WENDAL. Oh Mama. Why do you always defend him?

REBA. *(As if she didn't hear him.)* Oh me and Maybelle go but sometimes I think about what if ... what if something happened to your father ... he never wanted me to work. I ain't never been nothing but somebody's mother. And today I wondered if I had even been good at that. *(Wendal looks at her directly and she at him.)* I defend him for the same reason I defend you ... because you both a part of me. Now why don't you tell Mama what's bothering you. I let it go for a week but something's eating you alive, I saw it when you first walked through that door.

WENDAL. Nothing.

REBA. *(Firmly.)* I asked you a question. Don't let me have to ask you twice.

WENDAL. I haven't been well Mama. Been a little under the weather.

REBA. *(Relieved.)* Well, we'll just have to get you better. It's probably one of them flu bugs going around ...

WENDAL. It's not that simple.

REBA. I'll make an appointment the first thing in the morning with Dr. Miller and ...

WENDAL. Has he ever treated an AIDS patient?

REBA. *(Not registering.)* Oh, he's treated all kinds of things. *(What he said sinking in.)* A what?

WENDAL. I have AIDS Mama.

REBA. Well we'll just get you there and have him check you out.

WENDAL. Mama, do you ever hear what people really say? Did you hear me say I have AIDS?

REBA. No Wendal. AIDS, I don't know nothing about it. You ain't got that.

WENDAL. I do.

REBA. What I just say? I don't know nothing about no ...

WENDAL. I'm sorry.

REBA. Oh my God, tell me you kidding Wendal.

WENDAL. I wish.

REBA. Bailey ...

WENDAL. I haven't figured out how to tell him.

REBA. How? How did you get something like this?

WENDAL. I don't know.

REBA. *(Her anger and fear out of control, loud.)* What do you mean you don't know? You come home and you're dying of some disease and you don't know how the hell you got it.

WENDAL. I'm not dying. I have ...

REBA. Did you have some kind of surgery and they gave you bad blood?

WENDAL. No. What difference does it make how I got it?

52

REBA. You been lying to us. You been home here and you ain't said a word ...

WENDAL.   Every day I tried to tell you ... I practiced this speech ...

REBA.   I don't want to hear no damn speech. I want to hear how the hell you got this? You're not one of them ... that why you got so mad at dinner?

WENDAL.   Mama.

REBA.   No. No. I know you're not. You've been living with Simone ...

WENDAL.   *(Carefully choosing his words.)* Mama, you know that I never was quite right like Daddy used to say ... *(No response from Reba.)* Try to understand Mama. I have relationships with women and sometimes with men.

REBA.   No you don't, un-un. No you don't. You're my son, just like Junior   ... you're a man. You're supposed to ...

WENDAL.   Supposed to what? Be like Daddy. His world don't stretch no farther than this couch ...

REBA.   Boy, who the hell are you to judge anybody?

WENDAL.   Mama, it's not much different than you and Auntie May?

REBA.   What you say?

WENDAL.   It's not so different than how you feel about Auntie May ...

REBA.   How dare you? How dare you twist me and Maybelle's relationship into this sickness you talking. That woman is like a sister to me. You hear me? A sister!

WENDAL.   A sister that might as well live here. You closer to her than you are to Daddy.

REBA.   *(Enraged.)* You shut up. Shut your mouth. Shut your filthy mouth. Don't be trying to compare that shit ... my life ain't the one on trial here.

WENDAL.   I'm sorry. I just thought you might understand Mama.

REBA.   UNDERSTAND! How can a mother understand that? How can I understand that you're one of them people, that I raised a liar for a son ... I was so happy ...

WENDAL.   Mama, forgive me. I would've done anything to

spare you ...

REBA. Is that why you don't come home?

WENDAL. It's hard pretending.

REBA. You don't have to pretend with us. We're your parents ...

WENDAL. Yeah, right. Dad can't stand to hear anything about my life and where does he get off having Dwayne call him Daddy?

REBA. *(His last words lost on her.)* Couldn't you have given us a chance? Maybe we would have ...

WENDAL. *(Softly, tries to touch her.)* I am now Mama.

REBA. *(Shudders at his touch, sharply.)* Don't you tell your father. You hear me? I'll tell him. It'll kill him if it came from you. *(More to herself.)* I should've never let you leave here. Bailey told me ... said I kept you too close, wasn't no room left over for him ... he told me no good would ever come to you ... he told me ... *(Yelling.)* You better get down on your knees right now boy and you better pray, beg God's forgiveness for your nasty wicked ways ...

WENDAL. Pray! Mama, what in the hell you think I've been doing? I've prayed every night. I laid in that hospital bed thirty two days and thirty two nights and all I did was pray. You know how lonely it is Mama to lay in a bed that ain't even your own for thirty two days, nothing but tubes and your own shit to keep you company; what it is to bite into a pillow all night so people can't hear you screaming? No TV, I didn't even have a quarter to buy myself a paper. I tried to get right with your God, I asked him for some spare time, to keep me from pitching my guts every hour, to keep me from shitting all over myself, to give me the strength to wipe my ass good enough so I didn't have to smell myself all night. I prayed that they would stop experimenting on me, stop the rashes, the infections, the sores up my ass. I prayed Mama for some company. I prayed that somebody would get their room wrong and happen into mine so I could talk to somebody, maybe they would even put their arms around me 'cause I was so damn scared, maybe it would be somebody who would come back, somebody who would want to know me for who

I really was and I prayed harder and I prayed to your God that if I could just hold on, if I could just get home ... I'm not going to apologize Mama for loving who I loved, I ain't even gonna apologize for getting this shit, I've lived a lie and I'm gonna have to answer for that, but I'll be damn if I'm gon' keep lying, I ain't got the energy. I'm a deal with it just like you taught me to deal with everything else that came my way ... but I could use a little help Mama ...

REBA.   No more. You hear me Wendal? No more. I never thought I'd see the day I'd be ashamed of you, that I wouldn't even want to know you. *(She exits.)*

WENDAL.   *(Quietly to himself.)* Well, welcome home Wendal. *(Lights. The next morning. Wendal is still asleep on the couch. Dwayne enters from the kitchen.)*

DWAYNE.   *(Nudging Wendal.)* Daddy. Daddy. You woke?

WENDAL.   Hmm.

DWAYNE.   Daddy, you woke?

WENDAL.   I am now.

DWAYNE.   You want to watch videos?

WENDEL.   It's a little early, isn't it? *(Dwayne turns on the television.)*

BAILEY.   *(Coming down the stairs.)* I don't see why we have to go to Church today, it ain't even Sunday.

WENDAL.   Morning Dad.

BAILEY.   Morning. You feeling better this morning?

WENDAL.   Yeah.

REBA.   DWAYNE!!!!

BAILEY.   I don't know what's gotten into that woman this morning.

WENDAL.   Go see what your Grandma wants.

DWAYNE.   Ok. Granddaddy, I made you some toast. I left it on the table.

BAILEY.   Thanks, 'cause if it's up to your Grandma, I'm not getting nothing this morning. She in some kind of state. *(Dwayne exits, a moment.)*

WENDAL.   Sorry 'bout last night. You've done a good job with him.

BAILEY.   I tried.

WENDAL. It shows. *(Neither speak for a minute.)* Dad.

BAILEY. *(Overlapping.)* Son. *(They laugh.)*

WENDAL. Age before beauty.

BAILEY. *(Playfully.)* All right boy, I can still take you out. Only reason I ain't is 'cause I don't wanna mess up my Sunday-go-to meetin' clothes.

WENDAL. Dad, you'll never change.

BAILEY. *(More than a hint of seriousness.)* Do you want me to?

WENDAL. *(A moment.)* I try not to want for things anymore, 'specially things I have no control over.

BAILEY. Yeah, I guess that's probably wise. *(Another pause.)*

REBA. *(Yelling from upstairs.)* Bailey!!!

BAILEY. *(Yelling back.)* What? What Reba?

REBA. Are you ready?

BAILEY. Yes woman. Yes. I been ready. *(To Wendal.)* Now where were we? What were we talking 'bout?

WENDAL. You were 'bout to tell me you glad I'm home.

BAILEY. *(Looks at him for a moment.)* Why you trying to pick around inside me boy?

WENDAL. I wasn't. I was just ... forget it.

BAILEY. *(Pause.)* You know my offer still stands. If you ever want to come work for me ... I got a lotta plans for the store. Did I tell you I'm thinking about expanding?

WENDAL. Yes.

BAILEY. Not interested, huh?

WENDAL. I didn't say that.

BAILEY. Yeah.

REBA. *(Coming down the stairs carrying an overnight bag, overlapping.)* Look how nasty this table-cloth is. *(Whisks the table-cloth off the table, looks around trying to figure out where to put it.)*

BAILEY. Reba, the tablecloth wasn't that dirty. Leave it on the chair, we can get it when we get back.

REBA. I said it was nasty. I want it out of my sight.

BAILEY. Sugar, I don't know why you so upset but ...

DWAYNE. And I don't understand why I have to go to Aunt May's. I can stay here, clean out the basement. Dad and I can clean it out and get it done by the time you get back. Right Dad?

56

BAILEY.   That basement is filthy. Reba, if he's not going to Church, then why can't he stay here?

REBA.   FINE. WHATEVER YOU SAY IS FINE BAILEY. WHAT DO I HAVE TO SAY ABOUT ANYTHING AROUND HERE ANYWAY? WHAT HAVE I EVER HAD TO SAY ABOUT ANYTHING?

BAILEY.   I didn't mean it like that Reba. I just thought the boy might wanna ...

WENDAL.   Dwayne, why don't you go start on the basement while your grandparents and I talk.

DWAYNE.   But am I staying home?

WENDAL.   Yes. Now go. *(Dwayne exits.)*

BAILEY.   What's going on here?

WENDAL.   Dad ...

REBA.   *(Cutting him off.)* Nothing. Bailey, I wanna talk to Wendal. Alone. Please wait for me in the car. Please.

BAILEY.   Somethin' I should know?

WENDAL.   Yes.

REBA.   *(Overlapping.)* No. Bailey please. Please honey. And take the suitcase with you.

BAILEY.   *(Picks up the suitcase, mumbling to himself.)* A suitcase to church ... it ain't even Sunday ... all morning 'bout to take my head off, now I gotta go wait in the car like some child. *(He exits.)*

WENDAL.   Mama, I should tell ...

REBA.   Shut up. Just shut up. Don't say a word. I heard enough from you last night to last me a lifetime. I'm about to walk out that door and try and explain to that man out there why I don't have a home no more. I hate what you've done to my house Wendal. Spent my life here, inside these walls, trying to stay safe, keep my family safe ... didn't know any better, maybe if I had, I could deal with what you done brought in here. See this slipcover, I made it. And that afghan, I made that too, these curtains ... I made this table-cloth, see this lace. I made you. My son! And I took such pride ... but last night you made me realize I hadn't made nothing, not a damn thing ... been walking around fooling myself.... It's hard to look at something ... I mean I look

57

around here and it's like somebody came in and smeared shit all over my walls ... I'm scared to touch anything ... you hear me Wendal, scared to touch anything in my own house.... Nothing. Maybe if I could get outside these walls I could ... I can't stay here and watch it fester, crumble down around me ... right now I can't help you ... I can hardly stand to even look at you ... I can't help your father ... what good am I? I don't know anymore. I just know this house is closing in on me and I got to get out of here.

WENDAL. But Mama I can go.

REBA. Wouldn't make no difference. This ain't a home no more.

WENDAL. Mama, can we at least talk? I need you ... if you would just let me ...

REBA. You need?! Hmph! You need?!! I don't give a damn about what you need Wendal. Did you give a damn about us?

WENDAL. You act like I got this just to hurt you.... Don't leave Mama ... I ...

REBA. I can't help you right now. You understand? Mama can't help you. *(Starting to exit.)*

WENDAL. But where are you going? *(Reba exits. Wendal throws something, maybe hits the door behind her as his beeper goes off, he retrieves his pill box, gets ready to take his medicine but instead throws the pills across the room, after a moment.)*

DWAYNE. *(Enters.)* Dad, you ok? *(Wendal jumps.)*

WENDAL. *(Snaps.)* Man, don't come up behind me like that.

DWAYNE. I'm sorry. Can I ask you something? *(Wendal nods yes.)* I only need 'bout forty more dollars. Schools almost out and I thought I could go back with you for the summer. Simone said it was ok.

WENDAL. You talked to Simone?

DWAYNE. Yeah we were gonna surprise you. She said she was fixing me up a room.

WENDAL. Dwayne, Simone and I ain't together no more. So you don't have to pack up, your Dad plans to be around here.

DWAYNE. *(Excited.)* Really? Wow, then we could go places,

go to all the games ... Daddy, I mean Granddaddy, he takes me to the games and he tries to play ball ... don't tell him I said this, but he's kind of old ...

WENDAL.   You don't have to worry, I won't tell him that. *(Pause.)* There's so much I want to say to you, like be careful how you judge people, weigh a man carefully, you never know when you may get on the same scale ...

DWAYNE.   You don't want me to be like Granddad.

WENDAL.   What I want is for you to think for yourself, make your own choices, you know the kind you can defend, not with your fists but in your heart.

DWAYNE.   I got it. So what we gon' do today?

WENDAL.   Why don't you go work in the basement for a while. I'll take a shower, then we'll go somewhere, maybe to the Center or take in a movie ...

JUNIOR.   *(Entering.)* How come nobody woke me up?

DWAYNE.   'Cause you were snoring. Granddaddy say you sound worse than Amtrak.

JUNIOR.   Ok man. I don't want to have to bust no head today. Have to do you like I used to do your Dad.

WENDAL.   Why you wanna lie to the boy? Wasn't a day in the week that somebody wasn't going upside your head. Your Uncle always had a lotta mouth Dwayne.

JUNIOR.   Don't let him lie to you. Your Uncle spent all his time defending your Dad.

WENDAL.   *(Obviously there's some truth in Junior's statement.)* Dwayne, the basement's calling you.

DWAYNE.   Ok. But I wanna hear ...

JUNIOR.   I'll tell you if you wanna hear some stories ...

WENDAL.   The basement Dwayne. You can listen to your Uncle's tales later.

DWAYNE.   Ok. You gon' call me when you ready to go? *(Wendal shakes his head yes; Dwayne exits.)*

JUNIOR.   Where's the folks?

WENDAL.   Church.

JUNIOR.   *(Looking for food in the kitchen.)* Wait a minute. It's not Sunday. Well, maybe it's some type of social. Mama didn't cook? *(Takes the milk carton out and drinks from it.)*

WENDAL.   I don't think so. Why did you have to say that shit in front of him?

JUNIOR.   What?

WENDAL.   Defending me.

JUNIOR.   What in the hell is wrong with you Wendal? I was just kidding. What happened to your sense of humor? And I did have to kick ass because of you. I know what it is. You must not be getting none? Is that your problem?

WENDEL.   Drop it man.

JUNIOR.   Hey, I was just trying to make conversation. I can take my black ass back upstairs.

WENDAL.   Junior wait. I'm just a little uptight.

JUNIOR.   I can see that.

WENDAL.   Ok already. Next subject. Service seems to agree with you. You look good. Going to back to school when you get out?

JUNIOR.   Nan, I don't think so.

WENDAL.   Don't they pay for it?

JUNIOR.   Yep.

WENDAL.   So what's stopping you?

JUNIOR.   Correct me if I'm wrong, but I don't remember you going back to school.

WENDAL.   I know I didn't, that's why I'm trying to talk to you knuckle-head. Man, look at you, you got a lot going for you ...

JUNIOR.   Guess who you starting to sound like? Reason you can't get along 'cause you two are too much alike. And I sure as hell wish you'd stop using me in ya'lls battles....

WENDAL.   Man, what you talking about?

JUNIOR.   I'm not the favorite Wendal. Just your stand-in. God forbid you ever get your life together.

WENDAL.   I'll look over that last comment and deal with your initial silly ass statement. Dad's been throwing you up to me every since I can remember. If Junior did it, why didn't I figure out a way to do it better ...

JUNIOR.   Hit the nail on the head. Only time I count is when brother Wendal is fucking up ...

WENDAL.   I don't want to talk about him. I was just trying to tell you something for your own good. Junior you oughtta finish your education ...

JUNIOR. My own good is just that, my own good.

WENDAL. Man, your problem is you don't listen.

JUNIOR. Look who's talking. Seem to me, I listened better than you.

WENDAL. Not from where I'm sittin'.

JUNIOR. Well, you need to go sit somewhere else then. Look, I ain't trying to be you. Ain't into making no big in-roads. Call me Joe-Regular. Go to work, have a family, retire. Simple. I don't fault you for your life, so get up offa me 'bout mine.

WENDAL. I didn't mean no harm.

JUNIOR. Yeah right. As long as we straight.

WENDAL. Guess I was just playing big brother. Didn't mean no harm.

JUNIOR. *(Pause.)* Want you to be my best man.

WENDAL. Say what?

JUNIOR. Yeah. Yeah. When the right woman comes along ... what can I say? She teaches school, one of them fine church-going woman. Her name is A-nita and she loves my dirty drawers and Lord knows I can smell hers all day long, you hear me?

WENDAL. Man you crazy. *(They both laugh, it's a needed tension release.)* Congratulations Junior. *(Goes to hug him.)*

JUNIOR. Go on Wendal, you still ain't learned 'bout hugging up on men ...

WENDAL. I love you man, that's all.

JUNIOR. I know that ... we brothers. Man you been smoking some funny shit this early ... *(Wendal starts coughing uncontrollably.)* What's wrong with you Wendal?

WENDEL. Junior ...

DWAYNE. *(Enters.)* I need some garbage bags. Dad, I thought you were gon' take a shower? If we don't get to the Center early ... *(Bailey enters, it's obvious he's trying hard to control himself.)*

JUNIOR. *(To Dwayne.)* I don't think your father feels too well ...

61

DWAYNE.   What's wrong?

BAILEY.   Come here.

WENDAL.   What?

BAILEY.   I said come here. Bring your ass over here and look me in my face.

WENDAL.   Dwayne, go finish what you were doing.

BAILEY.   No, you don't. Stand right there. Don't you move.

WENDAL.   Dad, please, not in front of him.

JUNIOR.   Can somebody tell me what's going on here? Wendal come on ... let me help you ...

BAILEY.   *(Overlapping.)* Little late to be ashamed. *(Bailey roughly grabs and examines Wendal's arms.)* Where's your marks? Where you hiding 'em?

WENDAL.   What marks?

BAILEY.   You know what I'm talking about. You been doing drugs.

WENDAL.   Dwayne, get outta here.

BAILEY.   No. It's time he know the truth....

WENDAL.   I don't know what you talking about. Dwayne ...

BAILEY.   You don't know what I'm talking about? You don't know what I'm talking about!!! I'm one step off your ass boy ...

JUNIOR.   Dad, please he's sick.

BAILEY.   He's sick alright. Tell him. Let me hear you tell your brother, hear you tell your son, tell 'em you's a junkie.... Tell them why your mother was ashamed to stay in the same house with you. Tell 'em Mr. Junkie ...

WENDAL.   I'm not a junkie ...

BAILEY.   Then what the hell are you? *(The question hangs in the air, recognition, finally.)* I never laid a hand on you but you better get out my sight before I kick you straight to hell's door.

JUNIOR.   Will somebody clue me in?

WENDAL.   Dad, if you'd let me explain ... I'm not sure how I got it....

BAILEY.   I don't wanna know how you got it. The sight of you breaks my heart. I oughtta kill you. *(Shoves him.)*

DWAYNE.   Granddaddy, what's wrong?

WENDAL.   It's ok Dwayne. Go on now. Your grandfather is just upset about something.

JUNIOR.   *(Overlapping.)* Man stop it. Can't you see he's sick? I don't know what's going on here, but you gon' have to come through me 'cause I ain't gon' let you lay another hand on him ...

BAILEY.   Boy get out of my way. I'll go through you and anybody else. He won't need the AIDS when I get through....

JUNIOR.   What you say?

BAILEY.   AIDS. That's what I said.

JUNIOR.   Naw Wendal. It can't be. You ain't got that. Tell me you ain't got that.

DWAYNE.   Dad?

WENDAL.   Dwayne ... I'm sorry. If you all would just let me explain ... I didn't know if you'd understand....

BAILEY.   You right. I don't understand. You no son of mine. In my house.... Did you hear me? *(Violently throws Wendal on the floor, who attempts to crawl away from him.)* Take your sissy fairy ass and get the hell out of my house.

JUNIOR.   What the fuck you doing? He's sick. Look at him.

WENDAL.   *(Reaches out for Dwayne.)* Dwayne ... *(Dwayne backs off, exits.)*

JUNIOR.   Wendal why? Naw, I can't deal with this.... Can't deal with this right now ... I looked up to you ... I looked up to him ... I can't deal with this ... I ... I ... can't ...

BAILEY.   *(To Junior.)* Boy, stop that whining. *(Junior is crying, turns his back, walks away to exit.)* Did you hear me? Stop all that whimpering. *(Just before Junior is almost out the room.)* Where you think you goin'? You just gon' turn your back? Raised you to turn your back on your brother? *(Junior stops, but doesn't turn around.)*

JUNIOR.   Don't do it Dad ...

BAILEY.   I'm talking to you Junior. You a man or not? Are you a man or not?

JUNIOR.   *(Pause, finally turns around, he's crying.)* It's not gon' work this time. You hear me? It's not gon' work Dad. You got what you always wanted. Right there. He's all yours. *(Turns around to exit.)*

BAILEY.   Boy, don't you turn your back to me. Don't you ever turn your back to me.

JUNIOR.   Fuck you. Is that man enough for you? There's your son Dad. There's the man you always wanted. *(He exits.)*

BAILEY.   *(Pause.)* Get up. I said get up. Get up Wendal.

WENDAL.   I can't Daddy.

BAILEY.   *(A beat as the anger is replaced by grief.)* If you could've just told me. Wendal, if you could've just told me. If you could've just told me ... you my son ... what we gon' do? *(Eventually he drops to his knees, scoops up Wendal, maybe rocks him, cries.)* you my son ... don't cry Wendal ... don't cry, we gon' get through this ... we Bailey men don't give up, do we?... just you and me now. Oh Wendal I been waitin' ... waitin' so long for you to grow into somethin' ... you my son ... God help me ... what I got to wait on now?... *(Lights dim as attendants wheel hospital bed into the Bailey living room. Wendal is placed in the bed, maybe Bailey helps. IV is hooked up. Bailey exits. A passage of time — it's weeks later. Bailey enters carrying wood. He is a changed man: gone is the neat appearance, the sense of order and control. He drops the wood, then opens Wendal's saxophone case, crosses to the kitchen, retrieves a towel, forgets why he has the towel ... looks over at Wendal, retrieves and puts on rubber gloves ... cleans him up.)* You woke?

WENDAL.   Where's Dwayne?

BAILEY.   Maybelle's bringing him.

WENDAL.   Mama?

BAILEY.   *(An untruth.)* She asked about you. *(Turning him to check the bed pad.)*

WENDAL.   Really?

BAILEY.   Yeah.

WENDAL.   She coming home?

BAILEY.   Yeah. And she'll be sending your dinner after awhile ...

WENDAL.   I was gon' take him on the train with me. Remember when we took the train.

BAILEY.   Yeah. I remember. Look. I bought the wood in ... member for the cabinets? We can sand a little after you have your supper.

WENDAL. Look Wendal, you see it? That's red dirt ... sweet Mississippi dirt. I see it Dad. Mama, you see it? Mama?
BAILEY. *(Helpless, but with forced cheerfulness.)* You hungry? Maybe a little something. It was something else I was 'bout to do. Now what was it.... Oh I know. I was gon' clean up your horn for you. Shine it up, so you'd be real slick when you start playing again. Got to get this place cleaned up before your Mama gets home. She'll have my head on a platter, letting this house go like this. *(Starts to pick up a little: maybe strewn newspapers, mail.)* How 'bout a little soup? Couldn't get off to sleep last night, that couch ain't that comfortable, so I got up 'bout three with this bright idea. Thought I'd make you some soup ... cut up a lot of vegetables in it. *(Wendal moans.)* I know the sores hurt, *(Losing control.)* but how the hell you gon' get well if you don't eat somethin'? *(Recovers, less harsh, starts shining the saxophone.)* Yeah, I'll get this shined up for you. *(Blows a note or two on the horn.)* You wanna give it a try? *(Takes the horn to the bed, waits for Wendal to take, no response.)* Well, maybe a little later. Later on maybe you'll feel like playing, a little something. *(Places the horn on the table.)* Yeah it's a beautiful day outside. I wish you could see it. *(Crosses to the window, to himself.)* Your Mama likes days like this, she'd be out there in that garden right now wearing that funny hat with the fruit on it ... I got to figure out what I should put on to go over there. What you think? My blue suit or the black one? You wait a minute and I'm a go get 'em ... then we can decide. *(Just then Dwayne and Maybelle enter. Maybelle wears a hooded rain poncho, a wool scarf wrapped around her face and on her hands are oven mitts. Dwayne has a large bruise on his face; gone is the innocence, the sweetness; he's an angry little boy who doesn't know what to do with his anger, with any of his feelings.)* Hi. I'm glad ya'll got here ... just getting ready ... Maybelle, what in the hell do you have on? It must be ninety degrees outside. If you don't look ridiculous ...
MAYBELLE. I didn't want to take any chances. *(Looks around at all the things down in the house.)*
BAILEY. Maybelle, if it wasn't for ignorance, you wouldn't have no sense at all. And Dwayne what you hiding back there

for? Come over here. *(Reluctantly Dwayne crosses.)* Get over here! *(Notices the bruise.)* You been fighting? *(No response from Dwayne who looks at him defiantly.)* Did you hear me ask you a question?

MAYBELLE.   Them kids making that boy's life miserable.

DWAYNE.   I can handle myself.

BAILEY.   You try handling yourself some other kinda way. You speak to your Dad? *(No response from Dwayne.)* Boy get over there before that ain't the only bruise you sportin'.

DWAYNE.   *(Crosses to the bed, has a hard time looking at Wendal; begrudgingly.)* Hi.

BAILEY.   *(Takes Maybelle to the side.)* How's Reba today? *(Now that Bailey isn't looking Dwayne moves away from the bed.)*

MAYBELLE.   The same. Driving me nuts. Bathing all day and when she ain't in the tub she's somewhere changing clothes. I swear she ain't never been a vain woman, but now she hangs in that mirror for hours ... I don't know what she sees ... I wish she'd cry or yell or do something ... 'cause right now I can't reach her ... everyday she slipping a little further away from me. *(Whispers.)* Spends half the night watching Dwayne sleep. That's right, I'm telling you the truth, she sits straight up in that chair and watches that boy sleep, and then she goes in the room and the rest of the night she's walking and talking, to who I don't know, to herself or God one.... She misses you.

BAILEY.   Then she oughtta come home.

MAYBELLE.   *(Pause.)* Today's menu: chicken and fried corn. I tried to get Reba to help ...

BAILEY.   *(Taking the tin foil off the plate.)* This looks good. Wendal likes fried corn. Look Wendal.

MAYBELLE.   Bailey you know he can't eat that.

BAILEY.   How you know what he can eat? How do any of y'all know what he can eat? I been in this house with this boy for weeks and has anybody come by? Has anyone bothered to come and see what he can eat?

MAYBELLE.   I'm doing the best I can. I cook everyday for you ... I don't know what else you expect ... I'm taking care of Reba and that boy. Come on Dwayne let's go.

BAILEY. What you mean? Ya'll just got here. I was hoping you'd stay with him so I could go sit with Reba a while ... *(Wendal grunts, moans.)*

MAYBELLE. *(Timidly, waves.)* Hi Wendal. It's Maybelle, Auntie May. I can't stay ...

BAILEY. What's wrong with you? Even if he wanted to, he ain't got the strength to bite your ass.

MAYBELLE. It ain't no cause for you to talk to me like that.

BAILEY. And it ain't no cause for you to be afraid of him like that. Why don't you touch him ...

MAYBELLE. Have you gone nuts?

BAILEY. *(The cost of all the weeks of holding it together, he explodes; there's an edge of madness, grabs her, forces her to the bed.)* I said touch him. You used to rock him and sing to him, just like he was your own.... I want you to touch him ... right now ...

MAYBELLE. Bailey let go of me. You scaring me.

BAILEY. Good. Touch him. That's my son you treating like some leper. I said touch him.

MAYBELLE. *(Terrified, crying.)* Let me go Bailey. Let me go. I can't. Please.

BAILEY. What if it was one of your sons? Huh?

MAYBELLE. I wouldn't touch them either. I wouldn't have no AIDS in my house.

WENDAL. *(Overlapping.)* Dad, it hurts.

BAILEY. *(Quickly letting go of Maybelle, who retreats.)* I'm right here Wendal.

WENDAL. I wanna go. Help me. It hurts. I gotta go see Simone ...

BAILEY. Now hold on Wendal. Dwayne's here. *(To Dwayne.)* Say something to him.

DWAYNE. *(Still defiant.)* What?

BAILEY. Tell him you love him. *(No response from Dwayne, pleading.)* Please Dwayne. Tell him something. Anything. He's still your father. You may not get another chance.... He's still ... *(Dwayne doesn't move.)*

WENDAL. *(Overlapping.)* You see that plot of land, that's

where your old man first started kicking ...

BAILEY.   *(Panicking.)* Fight Wendal. Remember what I told you 'bout fighting. Don't let him take you out. Stay on the ropes son.... You can't give up. Come on. Don't give up. I'm in there with you. Ain't gon' let you go yet.... Come on son, fight now.

MAYBELLE.   I got to get out of here. I'll send Reba. Come on Dwayne. *(Dwayne doesn't move.)* Wendal, Auntie May love you. I'm sorry Bailey. I'm so sorry. *(She exits.)*

WENDAL.   *(Overlapping.)* I'm riding Dad. I'm on the train. I see you ... Junior. I see Dwayne ... Mama ... *(Simone enters in profile on the other side of the stage, a special light.)* Simone ... *(Gasping for breath.)* She's pregnant. Oh my God no ... I'm so sorry Simone ... I'm sorry ...

BAILEY.   I'm right here Wendal, but don't die on me. Please, don't leave me.... *(Bailey screams.)* NO.... *(Sobbing.)* Don't take him. Don't take him. God, give me some more time with him ... just one more day, please don't take him. *(Lights on Simone. Simone takes off her earrings, then her wig and then the robe and transforms into Angel Peterson from Act One.)*

SIMONE.   *(Fully transformed.)* God don't have nothing to do with it. Time to get on board Wendal Bailey. Welcome to the family ... *(As lights go down, Angel sings the same song Wendal was singing in the first scene in the reception area.)*

THE END

PROPERTY LIST

ACT ONE

Prologue
Saxophone with case (WENDAL)
Kitchen table
Cigarettes (DOUGLASS)
Matches/lighter (DOUGLASS)
Tablecloth (REBA)

Magazine (ANGEL PETERSON)
Small Table and chair (NURSE)
Appointment book (NURSE)
2 other chairs
Bag (WENDAL)
Book (*Tao Te Ching*) (WENDAL)
Clipboard with medical forms
Pen
Big bag (ANGEL)

Gift box with red dress (MAYBELLE)
Table and chairs
2 suits in dry cleaner's bags (BAILEY)
Nail polish (MAYBELLE)
Emery board (MAYBELLE)

Chair
Stethoscope (DOCTOR)

Phones
Speech cards (BAILEY)

Chairs (DOUGLASS, SIMONE)
Papers (DOUGLASS)
Pen (DOUGLASS)
Lotion (SIMONE)
Beer (DOUGLASS)
Receipt (SIMONE)
Brochure (DOUGLASS)

Futon cushion
Sheet
Cigarette and lighter (WENDAL)

Cassette (jazz) (DOCTOR)
Hospital bed
Night stand
Dressing
IV hook up and stand
Surgical tape (that does not rip hair)
Intercom buzzer (hand held)
Gifts: flowers (DOUGLASS)
          books: Bible
                  When Bad Things Happen to Good People
          candy
Speech cards (BAILEY)

Duffle bag (JUNIOR)
Small box with bracelet (JUNIOR)
Box with watch (JUNIOR)
Plaque
Jacket for Dwayne (JUNIOR)

Suitcase (WENDAL)
Wheelchair (NURSE)
Sax case (WENDAL)

ACT TWO

Dining table
6 chairs
Table setting for six
Purse (MAYBELLE)
Fork/spatula (JUNIOR)
Covered platter (WENDAL)
Pot with sauce (DWAYNE)
Casserole dish (WENDAL)
Covered dish (JUNIOR)

Medicine/pill box (WENDAL)
Glass of water

Suitcase (REBA)
Beeper (WENDAL)
Pill box (WENDAL)
Pills (WENDAL)
Milk carton (JUNIOR)

Hospital bed
IV unit and stand
Wood (BAILEY)
Saxophone with case
Towel (BAILEY)
Rubber gloves (BAILEY)
Newspapers (BAILEY)
Oven mitts (MAYBELLE)
Plate with tin foil (MAYBELLE)

SOUND EFFECTS

Applause
Phone ring
Hospital intercom

NEW PLAYS

★ **MONTHS ON END by Craig Pospisil.** In comic scenes, one for each month of the year, we follow the intertwined worlds of a circle of friends and family whose lives are poised between happiness and heartbreak. "...a triumph...these twelve vignettes all form crucial pieces in the eternal puzzle known as human relationships, an area in which the playwright displays an assured knowledge that spans deep sorrow to unbounded happiness." –*Ann Arbor News.* "...rings with emotional truth, humor...[an] endearing contemplation on love...entertaining and satisfying." –*Oakland Press.* [5M, 5W] ISBN: 0-8222-1892-5

★ **GOOD THING by Jessica Goldberg.** Brings us into the households of John and Nancy Roy, forty-something high-school guidance counselors whose marriage has been increasingly on the rocks and Dean and Mary, recent graduates struggling to make their way in life. "...a blend of gritty social drama, poetic humor and unsubtle existential contemplation..." –*Variety.* [3M, 3W] ISBN: 0-8222-1869-0

★ **THE DEAD EYE BOY by Angus MacLachlan.** Having fallen in love at their Narcotics Anonymous meeting, Billy and Shirley-Diane are striving to overcome the past together. But their relationship is complicated by the presence of Sorin, Shirley-Diane's fourteen-year-old son, a damaged reminder of her dark past. "...a grim, insightful portrait of an unmoored family..." –*NY Times.* "MacLachlan's play isn't for the squeamish, but then, tragic stories delivered at such an unrelenting fever pitch rarely are." –*Variety.* [1M, 1W, 1 boy] ISBN: 0-8222-1844-5

★ **[SIC] by Melissa James Gibson.** In adjacent apartments three young, ambitious neighbors come together to discuss, flirt, argue, share their dreams and plan their futures with unequal degrees of deep hopefulness and abject despair. "A work...concerned with the sound and power of language..." –*NY Times.* "...a wonderfully original take on urban friendship and the comedy of manners—a *Design for Living* for our times..." –*NY Observer.* [3M, 2W] ISBN: 0-8222-1872-0

★ **LOOKING FOR NORMAL by Jane Anderson.** Roy and Irma's twenty-five-year marriage is thrown into turmoil when Roy confesses that he is actually a woman trapped in a man's body, forcing the couple to wrestle with the meaning of their marriage and the delicate dynamics of family. "Jane Anderson's bittersweet transgender domestic comedy-drama ...is thoughtful and touching and full of wit and wisdom. A real audience pleaser." –*Hollywood Reporter.* [5M, 4W] ISBN: 0-8222-1857-7

★ **ENDPAPERS by Thomas McCormack.** The regal Joshua Maynard, the old and ailing head of a mid-sized, family-owned book-publishing house in New York City, must name a successor. One faction in the house backs a smart, "pragmatic" manager, the other faction a smart, "sensitive" editor and both factions fear what the other's man could do to this house— and to them. "If Kaufman and Hart had undertaken a comedy about the publishing business, they might have written *Endpapers*...a breathlessly fast, funny, and thoughtful comedy ...keeps you amused, guessing, and often surprised...profound in its empathy for the paradoxes of human nature." –*NY Magazine.* [7M, 4W] ISBN: 0-8222-1908-5

★ **THE PAVILION by Craig Wright.** By turns poetic and comic, romantic and philosophical, this play asks old lovers to face the consequences of difficult choices made long ago. "The script's greatest strength lies in the genuineness of its feeling." –*Houston Chronicle.* "Wright's perceptive, gently witty writing makes this familiar situation fresh and thoroughly involving." –*Philadelphia Inquirer.* [2M, 1W (flexible casting)] ISBN: 0-8222-1898-4

DRAMATISTS PLAY SERVICE, INC.
440 Park Avenue South, New York, NY 10016 212-683-8960 Fax 212-213-1539
postmaster@dramatists.com www.dramatists.com

NEW PLAYS

★ **BE AGGRESSIVE by Annie Weisman.** Vista Del Sol is paradise, sandy beaches, avocado-lined streets. But for seventeen-year-old cheerleader Laura, everything changes when her mother is killed in a car crash, and she embarks on a journey to the Spirit Institute of the South where she can learn "cheer" with Bible belt intensity. "...filled with lingual gymnastics...stylized rapid-fire dialogue..." –*Variety*. "...a new, exciting, and unique voice in the American theatre..." –*BackStage West*. [1M, 4W, extras] ISBN: 0-8222-1894-1

★ **FOUR by Christopher Shinn.** Four people struggle desperately to connect in this quiet, sophisticated, moving drama. "...smart, broken-hearted...Mr. Shinn has a precocious and forgiving sense of how power shifts in the game of sexual pursuit...He promises to be a playwright to reckon with..." –*NY Times*. "A voice emerges from an American place. It's got humor, sadness and a fresh and touching rhythm that tell of the loneliness and secrets of life...[a] poetic, haunting play." –*NY Post*. [3M, 1W] ISBN: 0-8222-1850-X

★ **WONDER OF THE WORLD by David Lindsay-Abaire.** A madcap picaresque involving Niagara Falls, a lonely tour-boat captain, a pair of bickering private detectives and a husband's dirty little secret. "Exceedingly whimsical and playfully wicked. Winning and genial. A top-drawer production." –*NY Times*. "Full frontal lunacy is on display. A most assuredly fresh and hilarious tragicomedy of marital discord run amok...absolutely hysterical..." –*Variety*. [3M, 4W (doubling)] ISBN: 0-8222-1863-1

★ **QED by Peter Parnell.** Nobel Prize-winning physicist and all-around genius Richard Feynman holds forth with captivating wit and wisdom in this fascinating biographical play that originally starred Alan Alda. "QED is a seductive mix of science, human affections, moral courage, and comic eccentricity. It reflects on, among other things, death, the absence of God, travel to an unexplored country, the pleasures of drumming, and the need to know and understand." –*NY Magazine*. "Its rhythms correspond to the way that people—even geniuses—approach and avoid highly emotional issues, and it portrays Feynman with affection and awe." –*The New Yorker*. [1M, 1W] ISBN: 0-8222-1924-7

★ **UNWRAP YOUR CANDY by Doug Wright.** Alternately chilling and hilarious, this deliciously macabre collection of four bedtime tales for adults is guaranteed to keep you awake for nights on end. "Engaging and intellectually satisfying...a treat to watch." –*NY Times*. "Fiendishly clever. Mordantly funny and chilling. Doug Wright teases, freezes and zaps us." –*Village Voice*. "Four bite-size plays that bite back." –*Variety*. [flexible casting] ISBN: 0-8222-1871-2

★ **FURTHER THAN THE FURTHEST THING by Zinnie Harris.** On a remote island in the middle of the Atlantic secrets are buried. When the outside world comes calling, the islanders find their world blown apart from the inside as well as beyond. "Harris winningly produces an intimate and poetic, as well as political, family saga." –*Independent (London)*. "Harris' enthralling adventure of a play marks a departure from stale, well-furrowed theatrical terrain." –*Evening Standard (London)*. [3M, 2W] ISBN: 0-8222-1874-7

★ **THE DESIGNATED MOURNER by Wallace Shawn.** The story of three people living in a country where what sort of books people like to read and how they choose to amuse themselves becomes both firmly personal and unexpectedly entangled with questions of survival. "This is a playwright who does not just tell you what it is like to be arrested at night by goons or to fall morally apart and become an aimless yet weirdly contented ghost yourself. He has the originality to make you feel it." –*Times (London)*. "A fascinating play with beautiful passages of writing..." –*Variety*. [2M, 1W] ISBN: 0-8222-1848-8

DRAMATISTS PLAY SERVICE, INC.
440 Park Avenue South, New York, NY 10016 212-683-8960 Fax 212-213-1539
postmaster@dramatists.com www.dramatists.com

NEW PLAYS

★ **SHEL'S SHORTS by Shel Silverstein.** Lauded poet, songwriter and author of children's books, the incomparable Shel Silverstein's short plays are deeply infused with the same wicked sense of humor that made him famous. "...[a] childlike honesty and twisted sense of humor." –*Boston Herald.* "...terse dialogue and an absurdity laced with a tang of dread give [*Shel's Shorts*] more than a trace of Samuel Beckett's comic existentialism." –*Boston Phoenix.* [flexible casting] ISBN: 0-8222-1897-6

★ **AN ADULT EVENING OF SHEL SILVERSTEIN by Shel Silverstein.** Welcome to the darkly comic world of Shel Silverstein, a world where nothing is as it seems and where the most innocent conversation can turn menacing in an instant. These ten imaginative plays vary widely in content, but the style is unmistakable. "...[*An Adult Evening*] shows off Silverstein's virtuosic gift for wordplay...[and] sends the audience out...with a clear appreciation of human nature as perverse and laughable." –*NY Times.* [flexible casting] ISBN: 0-8222-1873-9

★ **WHERE'S MY MONEY? by John Patrick Shanley.** A caustic and sardonic vivisection of the institution of marriage, laced with the author's inimitable razor-sharp wit. "...Shanley's gift for acid-laced one-liners and emotionally tumescent exchanges is certainly potent..." –*Variety.* "...lively, smart, occasionally scary and rich in reverse wisdom." –*NY Times.* [3M, 3W] ISBN: 0-8222-1865-8

★ **A FEW STOUT INDIVIDUALS by John Guare.** A wonderfully screwy comedy-drama that figures Ulysses S. Grant in the throes of writing his memoirs, surrounded by a cast of fantastical characters, including the Emperor and Empress of Japan, the opera star Adelina Patti and Mark Twain. "Guare's smarts, passion and creativity skyrocket to awesome heights..." –*Star Ledger.* "...precisely the kind of good new play that you might call an everyday miracle...every minute of it is fresh and newly alive..." –*Village Voice.* [10M, 3W] ISBN: 0-8222-1907-7

★ **BREATH, BOOM by Kia Corthron.** A look at fourteen years in the life of Prix, a Bronx native, from her ruthless girl-gang leadership at sixteen through her coming to maturity at thirty. "...vivid world, believable and eye-opening, a place worthy of a dramatic visit, where no one would want to live but many have to." –*NY Times.* "...rich with humor, terse vernacular strength and gritty detail..." –*Variety.* [1M, 9W] ISBN: 0-8222-1849-6

★ **THE LATE HENRY MOSS by Sam Shepard.** Two antagonistic brothers, Ray and Earl, are brought together after their father, Henry Moss, is found dead in his seedy New Mexico home in this classic Shepard tale. "...His singular gift has been for building mysteries out of the ordinary ingredients of American family life..." –*NY Times.* "...rich moments ...Shepard finds gold." –*LA Times.* [7M, 1W] ISBN: 0-8222-1858-5

★ **THE CARPETBAGGER'S CHILDREN by Horton Foote.** One family's history spanning from the Civil War to WWII is recounted by three sisters in evocative, intertwining monologues. "...bittersweet music—[a] rhapsody of ambivalence...in its modest, garrulous way...theatrically daring." –*The New Yorker.* [3W] ISBN: 0-8222-1843-7

★ **THE NINA VARIATIONS by Steven Dietz.** In this funny, fierce and heartbreaking homage to *The Seagull*, Dietz puts Chekhov's star-crossed lovers in a room and doesn't let them out. "A perfect little jewel of a play..." –*Shepherdstown Chronicle.* "...a delightful revelation of a writer at play; and also an odd, haunting, moving theater piece of lingering beauty." –*Eastside Journal (Seattle).* [1M, 1W (flexible casting)] ISBN: 0-8222-1891-7

DRAMATISTS PLAY SERVICE, INC.
440 Park Avenue South, New York, NY 10016 212-683-8960 Fax 212-213-1539
postmaster@dramatists.com www.dramatists.com